Second Night

Rajiv Dogra is an author, artist and television commentator. A career foreign service officer, he was India's Ambassador to Italy and Romania, the Permanent Representative to the United Nations Agencies in Rome and the last Consul General in Karachi.

An active public speaker, Dogra is one of India's foremost commentators on foreign policy and strategic affairs. He is the bestselling author of *Where Borders bleed*, regarded as one of the most authoritative books on India-Pakistan relations. *Second Night* is his third fiction novel, after *Footprints in Foreign Sands* (1997) and *Almost an Ambassador* (2005).

He lives in Delhi.

Second Night

RAJIV DOGRA

RUPA

Published by
Rupa Publications India Pvt. Ltd 2019
7/16, Ansari Road, Daryaganj
New Delhi 110002

Sales centres:
Allahabad Bengaluru Chennai
Hyderabad Jaipur Kathmandu
Kolkata Mumbai

ISBN: 978-93-5333-325-6

First impression 2019

10 9 8 7 6 5 4 3 2 1

The moral right of the author has been asserted.

Printed by Nutech Print Services, Faridabad

For my sister,
Dr Neera Ummat

Prologue

A red hot, flaming tandoor is my earliest childhood memory. Families like my father's, having fled from the newly carved Pakistan to settle in Delhi, would gather around the charcoal fired tandoor to have their rotis baked. I can tell you from my sweat-soaked experience that standing in the open, under the noon sun, next to a searing tandoor, is no fun.

But what was the alternative?

We were refugees who had to run away from our homes. Having left everything behind, we had to build new lives and start all over again. The once rich and the previously poor were equally miserable now; in one stroke, the division of India had made us one.

We were all staying in temporary, makeshift sheds. A private kitchen was a luxury we could only dream of, so the hot sun and the hotter tandoor had to be endured, day after day.

I was three years old then. I could not understand why a country had to be chopped up brutally, and the lives of millions of people disrupted abruptly. It is possible that people who were much older than me saw sense in all this cutting and chopping of human beings. But I doubt that, because their talk at the tandoor sounded angry and anguished. It spoke of bitterness, of killings, lootings, and missing relatives.

All this bewildered me.

Still, I pretended to be angry like them. Like others at the tandoor, I, too, tried to look hurt and anguished without knowing why I should be so. But even as a child I could sense that something vile had happened. People at the tandoor called it 'Partition'.

They were always shouting and raising their fists against the British—the angrez. But the deepest hatred and the choicest abuses were reserved for Pakistanis, because their insistence on a new country was the cause of our misery. Using swear words—like 'haramzade'—against them allowed men to let off steam into the hot air. But anger was no palliative—it could not revive the dead relatives nor get them back their properties.

Therefore, people, who gathered at the tandoor, were angry in short spurts and unhappy all the time.

Some of the older lot tried to pacify them by saying that even brothers fought and that divisions existed within families; properties, even single houses, were divided sometimes. So what if a wall had come up, making us two countries? The fact was that we were one people, we had lived together for thousands of years; our roots lay in Mohenjo-Daro's ruins, we belonged to the same stock, and we continued to be brothers.

This bit about brothers really riled people; it was like setting a cat among pigeons, like adding fuel to a raging fire. No one

RAJIV DOGRA

bought the brother argument. The majority of people around the tandoor shouted back, '*Thoo, thoo*, they are no brothers. One million people have been killed and you call Pakistanis our brothers!'

They were right to be angry because the world had rarely seen violence on such a large scale in so short a time.

But it was also a fact that we were, and actually are, one people. Our DNA is the same. Our faces, the colour of our skin, our way of thinking and our cultures are cast in the same mould. Geographically, too, we were one. It made no sense to separate us. But by drawing an arbitrary line the British had split us into two hostile nations. I could see, even then, through my young eyes, the trauma and struggle of people as they went about building new lives for themselves, and their frustration at the situation.

I could not understand the politics of it, but physically and emotionally, I was their partner in pain. I suffered with them. I, too, burned regularly in the summer heat as we waited for our dough to bake in the tandoor. My skin must have been very tender then—that is why it seared more easily than that of adults.

Back home from the tandoor—if you could call four walls covered in tin-sheet home—the four of us lived in a very cramped space. It sufficed only as a purdah to separate us from the world. My parents, my little sister, and I burned in the heat during summers and shivered in winters. In between, when it rained, we amused ourselves by singing to the musical tip-tap of the rain on our tin roof. The variation in the rhythm of the tip-tap provided the only variety to our miserable existence.

I felt for my sister and my parents. Why did they have to suffer, I used to ask myself even then.

You might contest that statement, and say that a three-year-old cannot understand such things. Perhaps you are right. I readily admit that I may not have fully comprehended the tragedy of Partition, or the fact that a million people were slaughtered and a million more displaced because of the whimsical decision of people like Mountbatten, Jinnah and Nehru. Even if I could not understand the more complicated things, I could see what was happening in front of my eyes—the remains of hands, cut off by Pakistani swords, and the tears of divided families for their missing relatives. The suffering of my own moved me even more.

My one-year-old sister cried every afternoon when the sun was unbearably hot. Years later, I can still hear her pained wails. Since our room had no furniture, she slept on the floor and spent her waking hours rolling about on the ground. Our mother kept a protective eye on her all the time, but sometimes when she was momentarily distracted, an ant would bite my sister. The poor thing would howl, but we could do nothing except to stamp on the ant in a tardy act of revenge.

This retribution did not lessen my sister's pain, or my anguish over it.

I also shared her pain when fever would make her delirious and we could not afford to call a doctor. Her cries would be like the screeches of a needle across my heart. They were the main reason why I spent most of my time out of the house—at the tandoor. I could not bear to see her suffer.

I could also feel the humiliation of my parents who had to

leave a prosperous home in Pakistan to live under a tin roof. I looked on enviously as the master of the big bungalow, whose servant's quarter we were occupying, returned every evening from his office to be greeted by a servant carrying ice-cold lemon squash on a silver tray.

I wished then that someday my father, too, would be given that respect. But it wasn't to be. Every evening he returned, a defeated man, to a sullen home.

He eventually did get a job. Later, we shifted to a proper house. It was not a bungalow, but it sufficed, considering the struggle of a new beginning. I have always regretted that circumstance and held my father's gentle nature against him. Had he been more ambitious we could have had a bungalow to ourselves, and he too might have been served cold drinks on a silver tray. But, as it turned out, these were big dreams.

In those difficult times, heat had become synonymous with poverty for me. The memories of that burning sensation continue to singe me even today. This is the reason why powerful air-conditioning figures in all my wish lists. My burning desire since my early childhood has been the same—that somehow I had to escape the Delhi heat. That must also be the reason why many chapters of my life were written in the cool Mussoorie.

one

$\mathcal{M}$ussoorie has always been a part of my life, but it is not the only thing that dominates my heart and mind. There are other, far more important, chapters.

Even now, after so many years, memories keep flooding my mind and I find myself going weak in the knees when I think of Sati. Those were the days when we walked as one on the tree-lined roads of Delhi University. She had the ravishing good looks of a film diva. Perfect strangers would stop her on the street and say, 'What are you doing here? You should be in Bombay, in films.'

Sati would simply roll her eyes and laugh it off.

When they saw us together, people spontaneously said that we wove magic. We were the perfect pair in a college known to breed lovebirds.

It was not as if we were anti-social and oblivious to everyone else in college. We had our friends; she had hers, just as I had mine. We would spend hours with our separate groups of friends, yet at the end of the day, it was us—just us together and no one else. We were in love, and we liked going out in the dark still night to hear the stars breathing. For us, we were each other's entire world. If it made us exclusive, that was for the world to decide.

Our ways were not those of the other careless youths. We were the nerds who never missed a class. Our debates made quotes, winning us most of the prizes. But every single rupee of that money was given away to support the poor students. It was Sati who insisted on it.

The moment one of us was given the prize money, she would rush to the student union office to deposit it in the fund for needy students. She didn't mind who they picked to support—her only condition was that our contribution had to be anonymous. 'I don't want anyone to feel grateful to us,' she would insist.

My dependence on her made other girls envious. 'Why can't you let us take charge?' they would complain to their boyfriends. The boys would nod but not listen to them.

This was not the only thing that set us apart from the rest. Every year, we were chosen as the most picture-perfect, made-for-each-other, and good-looking couple by the student's union. When we walked together, our classmates held their breath in awe. But I must be honest here and confess that this awe was inspired largely by her. When she moved, people did not see just another girl next door moving mechanically. There was the grace of a queen in her walk. She was royal with a big 'R', an angel with a soft 'a', and a heavenly spirit that floated like a feather across your eyes.

Once I told her, 'You are perfect.'

'Cakes are perfect.'

'You are flawless,' I insisted.

She laughed it off, but I had meant it sincerely.

I should also mention that throughout our time in college I remained true to Sati, and she to me. This isn't how it normally is because five years is a long time when you are young and restless. It can test the best of relationships. Some couples bicker and part, others switch partners—very few pairs last the full five years. It is all part of growing up where whims fashion impulse, making couples uncouple.

I do not think the idea of parting, or of straying, ever crossed our minds. It was obvious to everyone that we were besotted. That is why, together, we were known as 'Sat-Sati' in college, as if our names had been crafted to make us one. When we called out to each other, the tonal effect confirmed that impression. Sat and Sati sounded hyphenated, as if one was the echo of the other.

We were in love, and the world outside seemed to be in love with the idea of our love.

Long after we had passed out of college, succeeding generations of students continued to talk of our last day in college. Over the years, it acquired mythical proportions—like a modern-day Romeo-Juliet story or a Heer-Ranjha tale. It is still quoted in awed whispers as the proof of true love.

'How will you remember me?' Sati asked me on that last day together in college.

'Remember you?' I enquired, puzzled.

'Yes, how will you remember me?' Sati insisted.

'Why, why do you ask?' I said, stalling. 'The question of

remembering would arise if we were to part and go our separate ways. That's never going to happen.'

'Never is a long time,' Sati replied.

'Nothing is long enough for us. Not even forever.'

'Who knows?' she responded enigmatically. 'Life is so uncertain. We are here today, but tomorrow could surprise us. It is best to ask what should be asked when it must be asked. I will get to know then what you really think of me.'

'I could lie.'

'If you lie our love will die.'

We had never had a morbid conversation before this. For the first time in five years, I raised my voice. 'Sati! Never say that!' I said sharply.

Sati smiled, and looking coquettishly into my eyes, she repeated, 'Then tell me, how will you remember me?'

'I don't know. I have never thought of us in terms of growing apart. Honest to god, that is the truth.' I touched both my ears in confirmation. 'But what I know is this…'

'Yes?' she asked encouragingly.

'I know how the university would like to remember you.'

'How?'

'People would…like…' I wanted to say something nice, but I stopped midway, not wanting to complete what should have been easy to say.

This was uncharacteristic of me because I was not reticent by nature. Normally I was effusive and cheerful. My friends in college said that they could depend on me to come up with just the right words at all times, and under all circumstances. But for once, I was hesitant. I found myself reluctant to complete what I had begun to say.

Sati could sense my awkwardness. 'Let's go,' she suggested. 'I need a coffee.'

'We will,' I assured her, 'but I have to say this here, right here, in front of everyone.'

'Sat!' Sati said, puzzled.

'You know what people here want?'

'How would I know? There are so many of them anyway. It is difficult to get two class-fellows to agree on anything. How do you expect me to guess what hundreds of them may want together? They will never agree.'

'On this, they are all one. Everyone agrees.'

'And what might that be?' Sati was anxious to end the conversation.

'They say your eyes are the most beautiful in the entire university.'

'Shut up!' she shouted and tried to put her hand over my mouth to stop me, but I stepped back quickly to get out of her reach.

'They want you to gift your eyes to the university, so they can bewitch the coming generations.'

'Idiot!' Sati said in mock anger.

Suddenly, there was a chorus from behind the college gate, 'Gift us those eyes, Sati.'

A group of juniors had been hiding behind the boundary wall. They came over through the gate to join us. 'Sati, do that and your legend will live forever.'

Sati smiled shyly and pulled me away towards the coffee house. Behind us, we could hear the group of juniors talk about us, and of Sati's beauty.

'What was the need?' Sati complained. 'Now they will talk endlessly about it.'

'Let them talk, who cares.'

'I care,' Sati said bitterly. 'It is my reputation.'

A streak of red flashed across her eyes and jabbing an accusing finger at me, she added grimly, 'You are like Peter Pan who never grew up.'

'He won in the end.'

'Wrong, wrong, wrong!' she shouted, 'He lost the girl he loved. Wendy wanted to live freely.'

At this, I suddenly stopped in the middle of the road. Then, I bowed to her and bent down on one knee. After raising my right hand towards her, I began dramatically, 'Here, in front of the entire university, the college buildings, these trees and all the students, I am making a will.' I said all this in a voice loud enough to travel to the furthest ends of the road.

'Why are you shouting?'

'If I shout I can drown out all the doubting voices.'

'Stop it, please,' Sati pleaded, 'you are embarrassing me.'

'No, I must complete this. I want all of them to witness this.'

'To witness what, Sat?' Sati hissed.

'My will.'

'You are crazy, Sat.'

'Listen everyone, I say this in full consciousness. I, Sat, hereby will my heart and soul to Sati, because I love her like no man has ever loved a woman before.'

'Stupid,' Sati shouted and pretended to walk away.

'Wait, I haven't finished yet.'

'Enough,' Sati fumed, 'the entire university will know about it.'

'Good, I want them to know.' I laughed and began shouting at the top of my voice again, 'I promise before you all that whatever I earn in my lifetime will belong to Sati. Everything will be hers; my property, my stocks and my bank balance.'

'Your property! Your stocks! Your bank balance! Big dreams,' Sati couldn't resist stunting my soaring rhetoric.

Then, for no reason at all, she turned to walk back to her hostel. She was shaking her head slowly and I could hear her mutter, 'There are no happy-ever-afters. Just happy moments.'

I should have run after her and asked, 'Why? What has changed?' But as usual, I was late. I kept sitting in the middle of the road, watching her receding form.

Within the hour, my will was the big news of the university— various versions of it began to circulate. Over endless cups of tea and samosas, students added to the tale, making it more romantic and spicier.

It was this last act on my bent knee that turned our Sat-Sati saga into a legend.

$\mathcal{T}$he other legend in my life had lived in Mussoorie forever. Everyone in the little hill town knew her, yet her name, like much else about her, was a matter of guesswork for people. They tried hard to get it right when they met her first, listening carefully to the way she pronounced it. But mostly, they heard a clipped sound which started with a 'K' and ended abruptly with a sharp 'G'. Something like 'Kl...ng', though a few who had been to London insisted knowledgably that the name was pronounced as 'Keeling'.

Yet, to the vast majority, she remained Mrs Killing.

It is odd that a simple English name was difficult to pronounce in Mussoorie. After all, this queen of Indian hills had been a recuperation station for the ailing British soldiers for well over a century. Through the years, the local people must have heard hundreds of phonetically challenging names. And in the colonial times, you could get killed for making a Killing of Keeling.

Six decades have passed since the colonial times, and the

English soldiers have gone back to their motherland. A few British men and women decided to stay on, either because they liked Mussoorie or because they were fearful of starting all over again in England. By a strange coincidence, most of these people had easy-to-pronounce names, like White, Black, or Grey. Only Mrs Keeling's name was a challenge.

Then, there was the matter of respect. Though the local people addressed each other by their first names, like Ramesh, Mahesh or Suresh, they insisted on prefixing 'Mr' or 'Mrs' to the names of English people. It was difficult to explain this deference to Mrs White, Black or Grey because they were one of us now—ordinary Indians. Perhaps it was the colour of their skin that made all the difference.

People were courteous in other ways too. Mrs Keeling had pride of place in the postcard booklet about Mussoorie. Being the oldest foreign resident, her photo, with the incorrect spelling of her name, came before everyone else's. In that photo, she looked tiny and truncated—just like her name.

She hadn't always been like that though.

The really old remember her as a reasonably tall woman of regal bearing. When she entered a room, a hush of awe enveloped it. People dropped whatever they were engaged in, including their food and conversation. Instead, they focused all their attention on her. They noticed the walk first, a mesmerizing hip-rolling leisurely gait of confidence. Some old-timers said that its sensuous rhythm reminded them of the '60s hit song, 'Hippy, hippy shake...', and watching her walk, they could appreciate the spirit behind those lyrics.

Mrs Keeling may or may not have been aware of that effect, but she would sway rather than walk into a room, and her eyes would always dart about busily, scanning the room.

Finally, when she would settle down on a chair, she would do so ceremonially, carefully tucking the folds of her dress under her. That way, her clothes remained wrinkle-free. This carefulness was a lifelong habit with her. Some people said it was due to her parsimonious nature—she was saving on her laundry bill. Mrs Killing knew that a few catty types were making such comments; she was also aware of the others who made fun of her mildly eccentric ways. But she did not mind. By way of a retort to such critics, she would say, 'I do what makes me happy. I may make mistakes, but they are mine and I don't have regrets.'

Once, when I went to meet her, I let it slip tactlessly that she should correct people in the matter of pronouncing her name. 'It's an easy name,' I insisted. 'I see no reason why they can't pronounce it correctly.'

She laughed it off with a wave, 'That's just silly.'

'But no, Mrs Keeling,' I pressed, 'it can't be allowed.'

'They don't do it deliberately. Even if someone slights me, I do not hold grudges. There is no place for deathbed conversations in my life,' she replied calmly. 'Life is too short anyway.'

I looked at her in surprise. What did she mean by life being short? She was touching ninety after all. Was it then a throwaway comment, or was she referring to her own mortality?

She could see that I was puzzled. She smiled mischievously, and in that instant, her wrinkled face transformed magically, giving a hint of what she must have looked like as a vivacious teenager.

'You know, it hardly matters how they pronounce my name. I am nearly deaf,' she announced, surprising me again.

'But you don't wear a hearing aid?'

'I wouldn't dream of it,' she snapped. 'It makes a girl look old.'

'Oh,' I gasped, 'but you have to communicate.'

'That's not difficult. At my age, I can guess what people want to say.'

three

Mr Keeling had passed away nearly thirty years ago. Shortly thereafter, their two sons had left India to settle in the far ends of the globe—one in the USA, the other in England. She lived alone in Mussoorie—that was the reason I was visiting Mrs Keeling.

I had gone to school with her boys in Dehradun, and then we had stayed in touch during our college years. We had gone to different colleges, though; they had attended the engineering college in Roorkee to stay close to Mussoorie, whereas I had gone to a college in Delhi.

But that would make no difference to our holiday plans. During short breaks, like an extended weekend at school, and later at college, they would rush to the hills to be with their mother. I would invariably accompany them.

Nothing much had changed in the house since then. The colour of the walls, the sofas, and even the muffins we ate with tea were exactly as they had always been. It felt as if time stood still. Everything looked the same—elegant and neatly set. But there was one big difference from before—this time when I went there alone, the cottage was serene.

It would never be this quiet when we, the three ruffians, would visit her during our holidays.

Mrs Keeling must have been reminded of those times when her sons and I would outdo each other in hitting the longest ball across the valley, or in shouting the loudest into the void; something boastful, like, 'Wait, world, here I come!' We would ask Mrs Keeling to play the referee and judge who had hit the furthest or had shouted the loudest. She would invariably take my name, much to the feigned consternation of her sons.

She would be lying, of course, but this was how she was—considerate to the point of being self-sacrificing.

Her partiality drew me closer to her. That was one reason I came back to India, while her sons ventured forth abroad. But to be fair, even there, they worried constantly about their mother.

I wondered, however, about their method of communication. With her hearing being what it was, how could she guess what they wanted to know during their weekly telephone calls?

'With your sons? Isn't it difficult to talk to them without a hearing aid?' I asked her. 'Their voices must be faint.'

'No, not at all,' she laughed, 'that's the easiest part. At my age, their greatest anxiety is my welfare. They want to know if I have broken a limb while pottering about in these hills. Or, if I have decided to pop off without giving them notice. So, whatever they say at the other end, I keep repeating, "Yes, yes, I am fine." It is enough to keep them going till the next week.'

'Do you visit them?' I prodded conversationally.

'When they send the air ticket, I go. But it turns out to be very expensive for me.'

'How?' I asked, wondering how it could be expensive for her when they were sending the ticket.

'I don't like travelling by train to Delhi,' she explained. 'Wherever I go, I must take my laptop along. Since I doze off during long journeys, I am constantly worried that it might get stolen on the train. It is not the laptop that I am afraid of losing, but what is inside it. It contains the memories of my lifetime. So, I always take a taxi from Mussoorie to the Delhi airport, and that journey turns out to be very expensive for me.'

I nodded, comprehending the economics of it at last.

Before leaving, I kissed her warmly on both the cheeks and said in a voice loud enough even for her to hear, 'Goodbye, Mrs Keeling.'

She nodded back and said, 'Don't worry, I'll be fine.' Then, she kissed me on the forehead as she would her sons.

four

_____

The last time I went to Mussoorie, I stayed in a hotel despite her protests. I thought this way I would not be inconveniencing her; otherwise she would spend all her time fussing over me.

Naturally, I spent the evening with her. She opened a bottle of her favourite red wine and we sat in the garden to drink and dine. As usual, she did most of the talking. From time to time, she would check herself and tell me, 'Look, I am doing all the talking. You should also say something.' But without giving me the chance to open my mouth, she would carry on again.

The wonderful thing about Mrs Keeling was that despite her age and failing health, she could still drink me under the table. Then, mildly sozzled, she would converse on any subject under the sun. And she spoke clearly; I do not recall her ever slurring her words. Rather, the more she drank, the more fascinating her conversations became. That evening, she was in a nostalgic mood and told me stories from her early days—her flirtations and her crushes before she had met Mr Keeling.

She also told me that though she had always been as Indian

as the next person in India, she resented the tendency among Indians to stereotype people into slots—Anglos were flirts, Brits meant authority. Thus, if they mistook her for an Anglo-Indian, because of her colour and her knowledge of the Hindi language, boys would flirt with her thinking she was easy game. But the moment they would find out that she was a pukka English girl, the same boys would turn deferential. She would remain the same person but their attitude would change. The boys would get afraid of taking liberties with her.

She was dead right, as always.

Among her many qualities, the one I was most fond of was her wicked sense of humour. Sometimes people misunderstood it and called her a class-conscious snob. For instance, she was very fond of telling people that in ancient Egypt they thought the kings and nobles had eternal souls while their slaves had transient souls that ended with death. She would add with a twinkle in her eyes, 'My soul will live forever.'

A statement like this would leave a listener wondering. Was Mrs Keeling hinting that she was royal whereas her listener's soul was transient like that of an Egyptian slave?

That evening, Mrs Keeling insisted on teaching me how to recognize trees by their scents, the pungent perfume of eucalyptus, and the soft scent of pines. I protested, saying we should talk about the old days and enjoy the wine, and that we could have the tree talk some other day. But she was firm.

She said, 'Some things must be done while there is still time.'

I did not understand the reason for her insistence then. But as I was leaving, she asked, 'What will I be when I am dead?'

I reacted angrily and told her that she had drank too much wine. But the fact that she had posed such a morbid query continued to bother me till late at night. I was surprised that an optimistic person like Mrs Keeling was talking of death.

The next day, I was supposed to leave for Delhi after breakfast. But an anxious-looking man barged into my hotel room in the morning. He must have been running a fair distance because he was out of breath, but somehow he babbled, 'Mrs Killing…'

I arched my eyebrows in enquiry.

'Mrs Killing…' he repeated inarticulately.

Then, he waved both his hands in a frantic back and forth motion, suggesting I should hurry and accompany him. I could guess something was wrong with Mrs Keeling, because her neighbours knew me well and they had seen me visit her the previous evening. I wished they had chosen a more communicative representative to send to me, because the man's incoherence was only adding to my anxiety.

I got ready quickly and accompanied him. When we reached her house, he took me straight to her bedroom. Mrs Keeling's room was the sunniest of the lot, bright even on the darkest of days. She was lying on her back, her face lit from the light of the bedside table lamp, which she must have forgotten to switch off a final time. Her eyes were open, looking stonily at some distant object. But what held my attention was the expression on her face; it was of extreme serenity. I noticed her laptop. It was clutched tightly in both her hands.

When she was alive, Mrs Keeling had a scent—flowery,

mixed with a little sweet. That morning, I smelt something different—the smell of decay.

For the rest of the day, I remained busy with the funeral arrangements, leaving me hardly any time to marshal my thoughts. But the image of the laptop clutched tight in her hands stayed with me. In fact, the laptop was held so securely that I had great difficulty in loosening it from her grip. When I mentioned this fact telephonically to her sons, they were equally intrigued. Considering the importance she attached to it, they were keen that I should keep the laptop safe with me until one of them reached Delhi.

All through the journey back to Delhi, the physical touch of the laptop kept reminding me of her, and of its mystery.

Mrs Keeling had been fond of posing riddles when we were young, and I had the impression that she had posed a new riddle for us. I also felt that she had given me a clue to this latest riddle when I had met her. But on the last evening of her life, I had failed to catch that hint.

Could it have been a reference to her bank accounts, I wondered briefly. I dismissed that possibility quickly because all her bank booklets were kept neatly in a drawer. Maybe it was a script of the novel that she always wanted to write; some writers could be intensely secretive about their writing. Even that didn't seem likely because I found the handwritten manuscript of a novel on the writing table. Over the next few days in Delhi, I found myself thinking repeatedly about the secrets locked up in that laptop. My inability to guess its contents frustrated me.

Finally, both her sons arrived. Shyam and Shiv always stayed with me when they were in Delhi; my house was practically theirs. Between the three of us, there were no formalities. We turned into schoolmates the moment we slipped out of our shoes. Then, with our feet tucked under us on the sofa, or sitting on a cushion on the floor, we would talk of old times.

Mrs Keeling had died peacefully at a ripe old age. So, there was none of the trauma that is normally associated with such meetings. Still, we were sombre for the first few hours. Gradually, the talk turned to riddles and her delight in tying us up in knots. In the middle of all this, one of us—I do not remember who—started operating her laptop.

There were copies of the letters she had sent to various people, and there were some statements of monthly accounts. A few of her favourite songs from the '50s were also stored there. She had tried to get her novel published; her letters to about twenty literary agents were collected under the label 'Fiction'. Each of those twenty agents had responded politely, praising the submission but regretting their inability to take it up. Some wrote their client list was full, others claimed that the market conditions were tough and the publishers were reluctant to take on first-time writers.

One section in the laptop was full of riddles; she must have consulted this part to pose riddles to us. We smiled, thinking of her and her obvious pleasure every time she had us flummoxed. Then, just as we were about to switch off the laptop, we noticed another entry.

It read, 'I know my favourite son will be near me when I die.' That was it, there was nothing else.

We thought it strange that she should have waited this long to declare greater affection for one of the two sons. In her lifetime, she had been scrupulously correct, distributing her love equally between the two. Why had she decided to sow discord in the end? And who between the two was the chosen one? The question began to puzzle us almost as much as the riddles she used to pose during our younger days.

Suddenly, we noticed a small arrow on the screen; it led us to a photo of a smiling Mrs Keeling. Below the photo was a caption that read, 'Give up? As usual?'

Then, another pop-up emerged to lead us to a new page. There, the name of her favourite son was written—the one who she had predicted would be near her at the time of her death.

The lump in my throat was bigger than theirs.

five

$\mathscr{M}$rs Keeling had been extraordinarily kind to place me above her sons in her affections and I will forever remain in her debt. But before you form an exaggerated impression of me, let me declare candidly that I am an average person. I have had a moderately successful career and my personal life has been tinged with regret. These days, I introspect because I have plenty of time to spare. If you assume that I also speculate to pass time, you would not be too wide off the mark.

But my speculations are not just the feverish imaginations of an idle and sometimes anguished mind. My thoughts are lofty, and they concern mostly the epochal moments of history. I like to think of the past not just as it was, but as it might have been. Let me give you a few examples of what agitates my mind.

What if the bullet that killed the Austrian Archduke in Serbia had missed its mark? Would World War I still have broken out?

What if Lenin had died on the train that took him to Russia in 1917? Would there still have been a revolution in Russia?

What if Nixon had not gone to China? Would China still be the superpower it is now?

What if Princess Diana had married Sarkozy instead of Prince Charles? Would Sarkozy still have divorced Diana to marry Carla Bruni?

You would agree that all these are sensitive issues and each one of them requires careful thinking. That is why I approach my reflections with gravitas; my serious look is proof of the crushing burden I carry. But I must confess that I am not engaged in puzzling over complex matters of the world all the time. There are many occasions when I remain immersed in my own affairs. They need not be about anything earthshakingly serious, yet I end up being intensely involved. As far as my own feelings are concerned, I admit there is no fixed destination.

I am a bit of a wanderer, at times, like a person who has drunk too much wine. Just as his head spins because of excessive wine, mine does because it is chasing too many dreams simultaneously. Sometimes I feel that the impressionists may have been in a similar state when they made their sensational paintings. But there is a big difference in their view of the world and mine—unlike them, my view of life is not idyllic.

Still, I strive all the time for such a world.

When I am not busy shaping global destiny, I imagine myself living a life full of parties. This is a world where I may not be a king, in fact, I would not want to be one because being a king or having any sort of formal title means that you are required to perform certain functions and assume some responsibilities. That is constitutionally difficult for me because all my life I have rebelled against the establishment.

Since the system is hidebound, I am of the firm opinion that all work is repetitive. Only a genius can make an original contribution. I am modest and I know my limitations; I do not pretend to be such a genius. So, I see no reason why I should labour to produce results that already exist.

Why should I try to reinvent the wheel? Why should I wipe clean a street that has already been swept in the morning? Why should I spend time poring over tomes to decide a lawsuit? Why can't I simply tell the court to repeat the judgement that had been passed in a similar case previously? Imagine the money and manpower it will save. Since people are not ready for such a radical shift in their thinking, I am not willing to shoulder fake responsibilities. That is why I do not want to be a king.

Yet, I want more for myself.

I want to have the wherewithal to buy luxuries at whim, a fancy car one day, a grand house the next. I want to be indulged, pampered and spoiled because all my life I have slaved and saved for tomorrow—a tomorrow secure and safe enough to let me pass comfortably through the dusk of my life.

That, in essence, is the big difference between the historians and yours truly. Historians rearrange material which have already perished, whereas I mould the present for my future. In this kaleidoscope, I do not want to play the role of an eager beaver.

Let me give a concrete example of what I mean. I have watched musicians work their hearts out at orchestra performances. Along with hearing and enjoying their music, I have always made it a point to observe them closely. I take my opera glasses to music concerts and concentrate on their facial expressions. I see anxiety writ large on their faces, as if their life depended on the perfection of the next note. Yet, what is their reward for this high degree of dedication?

All they get by way of an acknowledgement, at the end of a superb performance, is a passing inclusion in the sweep of the conductor's bow.

I do not want to be one of the hundred-odd orchestra members. I would like to be the conductor himself, because I want to be the one acknowledging the applause. I am genetically constructed to occupy the centre stage. You can call me pushy if you want to, but I do not ever want to bask in the reflected glory of someone else's glow.

Since I am getting things off my chest, let me make another confession.

I am enough of a boozer to know the truth about alcohol; that the taste is a very ancillary part of the point. When I drink—I mean, every evening when I drink—alcohol diminishes my interest in detail but vastly increases my ability to think big thoughts. The gleam of another life becomes brighter, and my imagination races to demolish all limits.

I begin to dream of a life without responsibilities, where I am lying on the beach all day and listening to calypso music in the evening. As I told you earlier, dear reader, I am a modest man. I am content with anything grilled to go with my drink.

So, as you can see, my needs are limited even though my dreams make me soar regularly. However, there are two things that figure prominently in any wish list I make. In a way, they are mutually contradictory; if I have one the other is out of reach. But let me list them out for you, then you can make up your mind about how to resolve that contradiction.

I have stayed in the same city, the same street, and the same house looking out at the same view virtually all my adult life. My view leads me to another house from where I get a mirror image. It is the same view when seen from the opposite end as well.

If I look at her from my window, she looks back at me from a similar window, at exactly the same height, in her house. Every morning, at 10 a.m. sharp, I rush to open my window. Invariably, she is there, silhouetted like a Raphael portrait in her window. This has been our daily routine for the last twenty years.

I am not in love with her, nor she with me. But I am addicted to this view like others are addicted to their morning cup of tea. To that extent, she has been a great influence on me and on the way I look at the world. In that sense, our relationship often reminds me of autumn—mature, mild, beautiful and pure, but transient.

At the same time, I have another dream.

I want to own a grand house; I do not seek a palace but a large house with powerful air-conditioning to keep the Delhi heat out. This, then, is my quandary. If I shift to a grand house, there would no longer be a mirror view to look forward to any more. Yet, I am desperate for that house. The alternative, of course, is to live in Mussoorie.

six

The morning after Shiv and Shyam arrived, we drove up to Mussoorie. During the journey, they told me they were keen to sell the house before they left India. 'Who knows how often we will be able to come back now?'

'It can't be true,' I thought to myself. How could they sell this house—the one for which their father had made the down payment from his first salary? I knew this because Mrs Keeling had proudly shown me the receipt once. She had been sentimentally attached to the house, but her sons were not driven by sentiment. Home for them was where they lived at the moment.

I did not say anything, but they must have noticed my hurt look. 'Of course, we will come to see you. And you will visit us,' Shiv said quickly, trying to cover up.

'You will, won't you?' Shyam added.

I was not sure.

Mrs Keeling had been the anchor who had kept us together. Once the mother figure is gone, the bonding glue begins to thin.

People get busy with their own little worlds, wherever they are. I did not say anything, but it seemed to me that this promise of visiting each other was more in line with our earlier resolves—of staying in the same city, of setting up a joint business company, of taking up a house and living there together.

When we were young, we would also talk about books, and even more about the books we were going to write. In the end, none of us ever got down to writing a book. So, this latest promise of theirs, of visiting each other, was built on a record of non-performance.

It was a sobering thought, and to be frank, I spent the rest of the journey wondering why I had invested so much in this friendship.

Meanwhile, it had started to rain, not in huge dollops, as is normally the case in the hills, but in gentle drops. Therefore, it was not the noise of the falling rain, but the screech of the car's wipers against the windscreen that brought me back to the real world. Looking out of the car window, I saw the passing street lights reflected in rainwater. They were of all shapes and sizes, some perfectly formed, others distorted—as in life.

By the time we reached Mussoorie, the sun had come out to wrap the town in its soft, golden glow. Once we had unpacked, there was nothing much to do till the time we met for the sundowner. Sitting alone in my room, I found myself thinking of the casual manner in which they had told me they were going to sell the Mussoorie house. To make it worse, they had heartlessly added, 'You will visit us, won't you?', as if I was desperate to cadge an invitation from them.

I kept fretting over it till I was struck by an odd whim. I wanted to go out alone and revisit all the places Mrs Keeling used to take us to. It turned out to be a long walk, much longer than I had planned. It was quite adventurous too, in the way the day shaped up. I skirted the chaos at the Library Point and hurried through the narrow mall road, before slowing down at the steeper slope leading up to Landour. That is when I began to reflect.

Some people, when they are offered heaven, moan that it is shackled to hell. Others view it as guarantee that they can have ecstasy at will. Landour is not heaven, it is not even heaven-like. In fact, this quaint little place has many shortcomings—that is why opinion is divided over where it really belongs.

Some fault it for being remote, away from all action, because the mall and the good restaurants are located in Mussoorie. Others differ; they say exclusivity is the point. And what a huge difference two thousand metres can make!

Mussoorie is crowded. In the peak summer season, there is hardly any walking space, and on weekends, there are so many people that they crash into each other on the mall road. It is noisy and becomes noisier still when fights break out over walking space. In the midst of this cacophony, tiny ponies have to negotiate their path as they transport the old and the very young from one end of the mall to the other. If you are not careful, you might step over the pony droppings that the mall is littered with all through the day. If you go beyond the mall and look down at Mussoorie from a height, the haphazard spread of its rooftops is hardly the stuff that inspires great paintings.

In contrast, Landour, which lies further up, is serene. But the hoi polloi rarely bother taking the steep, narrow road up to it merely for the satisfaction of breathing in the pine-scented air, and to walk through its tree-lined paths. They are more at home with the noisy and nosey Mussoorie crowd.

Therefore, depending upon your point of view, you could patronizingly say that Landour looks down on Mussoorie, or graciously maintain that Mussoorie looks up to the higher-placed Landour. Businessmen and bureaucrats live in Mussoorie, as it is convenient for them. Writers, actors and artists live in Landour; its isolation triggers their creative juices.

I should admit that this knowledge about the two places was given to me by Mrs Keeling. She had also told me about Hari, who fell between these two extremes.

Like his name, he could belong to both places. To Indians, he was Hari, which is another name for Lord Krishna. For the anglicized, he was Hari with a sharp 'a', as in Harry of England. If you asked him for his preference, he would say non-committedly, 'They are both the same for me'. But in his heart of hearts, he was a Harry; he would be happier whistling a Beethoven aria than be caught singing a Hari bhajan.

As an ex-headmaster of a boarding school, he could have settled in Mussoorie. A public schoolmaster would not be out of place in the company of bureaucrats and businessmen because their children formed the majority in these schools. But Hari considered Mussoorie intellectually stultifying. He was drawn instinctively to artists; his greatest desire was to write the ultimate Indian novel.

However, there was a practical problem—successful artists those days had deep pockets, therefore, land in Landour was expensive. But as Hari was only an aspiring writer, he had to settle for a plot of land between Mussoorie and Landour, where he could belong to both worlds—Mussoorie for good homely food and Landour for food for thought. One more thing must be said about Hari—he had not changed over the years.

At school, he was constantly busy, preoccupied with some great undertaking or the other. The air of serious purpose about him added to his aura, and this act must have worked because successive classes of graduating students remained in awe of him. Some continued to keep in touch long after passing out of school, seeking his steady hand to guide them in adult life too.

Mrs Keeling had told me a lot about him—in fact, almost everything that she had picked up from her social circle over the years. They were the sort of nuggets that help you form a picture of a person even before you meet him. For example, he was fond of boasting. After a whisky or two, he would say he knew many secrets about people—'If I put them all down on paper, my novel will be a bestseller.'

Like in school, in his retirement too, he maintained a rigorous routine. He would sit in front of his computer with the first morning light and keep on typing busily at it for the better part of the day. His intense concentration gave the impression that he was engaged in some momentous undertaking.

As a daily witness to his master's labours, his cook-cum-driver would remain duly deferential, hoping that one day he too might bask in the glory that was sure to come his master's way. If god was kind, and all went well, he would perhaps even get a part in the movie version of that book. Hari would often promise to put in a good word for him with the movie director. While Hari would sit stoically before the computer all day, his loyal cook-cum-driver would stand guard at the door so that no one disturbed his master at work.

Hari had been writing that book for years.

It was as a writer that he was introduced to me once. We were still in school and Shiv and Shyam were sulking for some reason, so they refused to accompany Mrs Keeling on her daily walk. To spite them more, Mrs Keeling took me to Landour for lunch. I was about sixteen and tall enough to tower over her as we walked together on the crowded mall road.

Though, at sixteen, I was too young to think about the sensitivities of a man-woman relationship, Mrs Keeling was always giving me little bits of advice about women. It was never a lecture about relationships, but more like stray thoughts from her experience. That day, as we were walking down the mall, she said, 'Being macho does not mean that a woman is inferior to you.'

Then, she stopped in the middle of the road and stood on her toes to tap me on the shoulder. I was looking down—it was a habit to look for potholes or pony droppings on the road—but she took offence. 'When a woman talks, you must acknowledge her. A woman likes to be noticed,' she reprimanded.

Having said that, she started walking again, as if the slight annoyance was a thing of a long-forgotten past. This had been one of the many qualities that I had admired about her—she did not hold grudges. I was also proud of the fact that invariably people would stop to greet Mrs Keeling. Little did I know that the respect was for the colour of her skin—a white person continued to represent imperial authority to the common man in India.

The first question I asked her at the restaurant was why she hadn't moved back to England when everyone else in India regarded a visa to England as a ticket to heaven.

She smiled mysteriously. Then, waving her hands towards the gathering mist in the valley below, she said, 'Listen, my child, there is nothing like this in the world. No other country offers more rapture than India. No other place fascinates in such depth and variety, with such horror and beauty, enchantment and frustration. No other place is so approachable and so utterly other. India is the most gregariously complex country in the world. I will never leave it.'

I was too young to fully comprehend these big words, but everything she said during that lunch sounded significant.

Later, as we were leaving the restaurant, she introduced me to Hari. She said he was the principal of a famous boarding school in Dehradun who had taken to writing after retirement. I was greatly impressed that I had actually met an author. That day, I walked back home with a spring in my step, hoping that the mere touch of Hari's hand would turn me into a writer.

Our first meeting at the restaurant had been far too brief for either of us to remember the other person's face. Therefore, a chance encounter on my way up to Landour that day was technically a meeting of strangers. Even the second time, Hari made only a cameo appearance, but it was long enough to fill me with excitement, entertainment and surprise.

I must have been standing on the midpoint between Mussoorie and Landour. Suddenly, a rough-looking man rushed down the road in agitation.

'Did you see her?' he wailed, giving imagination to my thoughts. I half-expected to see his dishevelled wife leaping off a cliff in great anger.

I began to look around anxiously but I could not see any woman, nor did I hear the rush of feet against loose rubble, which is a familiar prelude to the fatal jump they show in Bollywood movies. Since I had never seen anyone committing suicide before, I expected real life to imitate reel life, a faint rumble of rubble before the leap and the shriek—aiyeee or gaiyeee— depending upon the state of the mind of the jumper.

'It is my fault really,' he continued, adding to my suspicion.

Looking at him, I was not surprised that his wife had decided to jump.

His haphazardly tucked-in shirt was half-hanging out of his pants. His hair was unkempt, his body odour was stale, and he looked dirty. The shadow on his face was not the careless forgetfulness of one morning, but the result of boozy neglect of many days. His untidy half-beard made him look fierce.

'I wish I had rushed the moment I heard the noise,' he lamented. 'I could have stopped her.'

This caring sentiment softened me a bit; perhaps he was not the devil he appeared to be. Maybe he was genuinely sorry that his wife had left in a huff. I felt bad that I had judged him hastily.

Perhaps she was equally to blame. Maybe she was a shrew who had driven him to alcohol. It is difficult in the best of circumstances to guess what goes on behind the four walls of a house. Sometimes even people living under the same roof cannot say with any degree of certainty that only one or the other is the guilty party. So, how could a complete stranger like me guess what was wrong with them?

All this while, we had been walking up the hill towards Landour. Hari had kept a brisk pace, but there was none of the heavy breathing which slows down a city man. I, on the other hand, was tiring visibly. My legs were heavy and my thumping chest was beginning to ache.

'Come,' he insisted, 'let me show you the house of the greatest romantic hero of all time.'

It was just five hundred metres away, but there were five bends in the road and another climb of at least a hundred feet. I was panting by the time I stood in front of the crumbling structure.

'This thespian is obviously out of work,' I joked.

'No,' Hari said sharply, taking offence, 'Dev Anand was never out of work. He remained evergreen throughout his life. Millions of people imitate his style—and what a style he had!'

'He wobbled on flat roads,' I smirked. 'His legs were bent crookedly as if he was perpetually climbing some hill. And that head of his leaned like…' I faltered a bit, looking for the right word, '…like the Leaning Tower of Pisa; a walking, talking Leaning Tower of Pisa.'

Hari must have been a great fan of Dev Anand because my description embarrassed him. He shuffled nervously and contorted his face in confusion.

'Don't say that, he was a great man,' Hari said defensively. 'When he was a young star he was so good-looking that he was photographed more than his leading ladies. He mesmerized people. Finally, his film producers forbade him from wearing black clothes.'

'Why did they do that?'

'They told Dev Saheb that even when he wore ordinary clothes he outshone his heroines on screen. Imagine the effect he would have if he were to start filming in dark-coloured clothes. He was that handsome.'

'But this house,' I pressed, 'it must have seen better days.'

The house was surrounded by high walls, probably designed for privacy when Dev Anand was a mega star. Its red façade gave the impression of an owner who must have liked taking a spin in an open-top red car with the passing fancy of the moment. Now the paint on the boundary wall was peeling off, not in the deliberately unfinished way of Italian houses, but because of neglect over time.

'No one remembers the last time he used this house,' Hari

explained. 'He was a fairly regular visitor when his children were going to school here. But that was a long time ago.'

I was a bit of a fan of Dev Anand myself. As Hari put it, the man had style. Like millions of my generation, I too imitated his mannerisms—that toothy smile, the wobbly way of walking, and the exaggerated shake of head every time he finished a sentence. In my college days, I had spent hours in front of the bathroom mirror, trying to perfect the Dev Anand style.

On an impulse, I decided to invite Hari to the bungalow. 'What are you doing this evening?' I asked, vaguely.

It caught him by surprise. Since the context was not clear, he said, 'Nothing.'

'Come over for dinner then.'

'Oh, I don't know. I have this novel to get back to. It's a lot of work, really.'

'It will be nice if you can come. We have a bottle of malt to kill, it will be more fun together.'

The malt tempted him. He shifted from one foot to the other in indecision, wondering if he should accept a last-minute invitation from a stranger. In the end, the malt won.

'You are the visitor. I should be inviting you,' he resisted weakly.

'My friends are with me,' I said, 'and we are well cared for at the bungalow. The food should be good too.'

We shook hands and parted. However, throughout the long walk back, I kept wondering about his wife. It intrigued me that he had accepted an invitation for dinner on the very day that his wife had jumped off a hill.

eight

A ll these years I have recalled Sati's words like a guru mantra—
'Life is not an easy walk.' She was absolutely right because life is
difficult and full of unexpected turns. For instance, who could
have anticipated the sharp twist in our tale?

I also remember that once she had said, 'Let little ribbons
of memory, of what we have done together, remain with us.
Who knows where our lives might take us?'

I had protested, saying we would always be together, but
she had smiled mysteriously and said, 'Someday we will part.'

'Part? Some day? You have already decided that?' I had
reacted gloomily. 'Then, what are we doing sitting together,
pretending to be in love?'

'Does love actually exist?' she had asked, 'Or is it just a
fantasy made up by poets?'

This was how quick she was at repartee. Her responses often
left me feeling witless and tongue-tied, even though I was an ace
debater in college. She was not obsessive about talking all the
time. Instead, she would twirl one end of her dupatta around

her little finger to avoid saying something. That day, she had twirled her dupatta around her finger endlessly, sending out the message that she was undecided—about us, about herself, and about the future.

But I had failed to read that signal.

'She was a real stunner. There was a queue of boys wanting to marry her. Did she walk out on you? Was there someone else? I cannot understand this. This is the most horrible news we have heard in a long, long time,' Shiv said suddenly, bringing me back to the present. We were in the house, spending the evening together.

He was mercurial. His face mirrored his emotions faithfully; the odd wart showed easily. Usually, he gave the impression of a person who was less than solid, a bit incomplete, someone who was not soldered together seamlessly. Let's say he was not the kind of person who wanted to make his mark; his only wish was to live an unremarkable life full of pleasure and comfort.

His sharp reaction was quite in character. It was also true that both brothers were partial to Sati since the first time they had met her in the college café.

I remember that meeting well because I had felt proud showing off my girlfriend to Shyam and Shiv. Incidentally, the feeling of pride was even greater because they were yet to acquire girlfriends, and when you are in college, such firsts are important. Moreover, there was a look of completeness between Sati and me—it was the look that first-time lovers have.

All this was enough to unsettle anyone. But a truly beautiful woman unnerves people. They are either mesmerized and keep looking furtively at her, or they react uncharacteristically and say something silly. The same thing happened that day as well.

Within minutes of meeting her, Shiv blurted, 'You must come to Mussoorie with us. Our mother decides all our affairs, of all three of us, I mean.' He had included me in the generous sweep of his arm—'She will be delighted to meet you. I'm sure she will approve.'

'She will what?' Sati screamed, startling the other students at the café. 'Excuse me—I don't even know you guys.'

Her cheeks were flushed, and she slid back her chair to get up and go. But I held her hand and pleaded with her to stay. That was their first and last tiff. Later, it became a joke between them.

After that initial awkwardness, they got along like a house on fire. They used to banter constantly. One day, at the same café, Shiv was in a gregarious mood.

'Love can be selfish,' Shiv suggested, looking pointedly in my direction, 'but friends are forever. You accept things from a friend that you reject from a lover. Am I right?'

Sati smiled. She kept folding and unfolding her napkin as if seeking inspiration through the repetitive action. At last she found the words she was seeking, 'What you say is soufflé, untroubled by substance.'

'The entire point of soufflé, my dear Sati, is its fluff,' Shiv responded quickly.

'Really?' Sati replied. 'Then clearly what you and I hear are different. You hear the sounds of closing doors.'

'No, I hear the sounds of doors that open,' Shiv asserted in a voice far louder than he had intended. Then, softening his tone, he asked her again, 'Now, dear lady, since we are talking of opening doors, will you travel with us to Mussoorie?'

She was about to say something, maybe even a 'no' again, but Shyam stepped in, 'Please don't say no.'

The following weekend, she travelled with us to Mussoorie.

We took a train to Dehradun. From Dehra station, it was a short bus ride of about 30 km up the hills to Mussoorie. But to impress her, we decided to hire a taxi. It was an old fiat, the kind where the front seat is not divided into two. Shyam sat in front. Shiv, too, could have squeezed in there but he chose to sit at the back with us. Sati sat in the middle, I was to her right, and Shiv was pressing against her on the left. In the middle of the journey, I noticed Shiv slither his right hand up, across the back of Sati's seat. I had expected her to react, but she did not seem to mind.

When we reached Mussoorie, Mrs Keeling was effusive. She welcomed Sati into the house, saying, 'Now my house has four aces.'

'How?' we asked curiously.

'Simple. Sat, Sati, Shiv and Shyam. All your names start with "S". And in these parts, "S" sounds like an "ace". Voila! So I have my four "aces."'

Mrs Keeling was being nice as usual. But the fact was that in Mussoorie and its surroundings, people were more likely to pronounce 'S' as 'ass' rather than as 'ace'.

Sati left for Delhi on Sunday afternoon; I stayed back for another day.

After she had boarded the bus, Mrs Keeling remarked that

it was the most enjoyable time she had ever had. But when I asked her if she had liked Sati, Mrs Keeling replied mysteriously, 'You must always remember that we live in different worlds; we have different logics. Your truths are absolute and beautiful to you and her truths will be absolute and beautiful to her. Give her space.'

I nodded, but Mrs Keeling had not finished yet. 'Remember always that love demands letting go. If sacrifice is true love, then freedom, not possession, is true happiness.'

At that time, I did not have the patience to acknowledge this profound difference; to me love meant absolute merger, where two bodies became one soul. Mrs Keeling's was a different interpretation, but I was happy that she approved of Sati.

I was lost in that memory of Mrs Keeling and Sati, when Shyam interrupted me, 'What went wrong?'

'This is horrible,' Shiv added.

They had put me in the guilty corner, and I was acting the part. My eyes bore holes in the ground beneath my feet and my long face reflected the hopelessness of my situation.

'Come on, you have to tell us,' Shyam insisted.

I had no intention of hiding the truth from my closest friends. My reluctance was purely emotional. I feared I would break down midway through the narration. That, along with a bit of confusion about where to start and how much to tell, had held me back. Besides, with the passage of time, a lot that I needed to tell had accumulated.

There were many silences to be broken.

Since time and distance might have blurred their memory of

her and of our relationship, I decided to make it a full narration. Moreover, they had gone to a different college in a different city, so they were not aware of all the details of our relationship.

That day, in Mussoorie, I was going to tell them the complete story of my love. But before I could do that, Hari arrived.

$\mathscr{T}$he doorbell rang precisely at seven. I opened the door to a handsome man, smelling strongly of cologne. His transformation was so complete that I was about to ask if we had met earlier. Hari had shaved, shampooed his hair, and had obviously taken special care to comb them. What's more, he was dressed nattily in a black suit with a red tie. This time, his shirt was tucked smartly in his trousers.

I was wearing an open-neck shirt and chinos. I shook his hands warmly and took him to the lounge, but all the while I was wondering if this was how all recently widowed men behaved.

Hari looked immensely pleased with himself, and the spring in his step suggested that he was in a celebratory mood.

'Do you take ice?' I asked, pouring a generous helping of malt for him.

'No, thanks. I like my malt warm, like a young woman.'

'Some soda then?'

'Good heavens, no. I wouldn't dream of it. It's like diluting love.'

As we drank, our conversation became freer. He had already been boastful in the afternoon when we had first met, now he was soaring. After years of mesmerizing young men, he had acquired a conversational swagger.

He became chattier in front of Shiv and Shyam. Hari shook hands with them vigorously, and acknowledged that he had met their mother once. That was the only interruption in his flow.

'I like to keep in touch,' he said apropos nothing at all. 'I don't chase them, but many of my ex-students still seek me out. If they have a problem in their job or a crisis at home, they turn to me. I just make sure that I am available to them with all the experience at my command. This is what I promised every graduating class, that I will be there when they need me. They just have to yell. It's a two-way street, you know, they respect me and I keep their trust.'

He paused for a sip of his drink, a long sip actually. Then he saw the kebabs. I thought I could notice a glint in his eyes, but he turned away quickly when he saw me noticing his hungry look. At first, when I pushed the kebab plate towards him, he said no. But when I insisted, he agreed to take one.

I slid the kebab plate a little more towards him and turned to refill our glasses. All this must not have taken more than a few seconds but when I leaned forward to place his drink on the table in front of him, I noticed the pile of kebabs on his plate. I had never seen a guest so hungry before. It was as if he had not eaten for months.

Shiv and Shyam had also noticed the small mountain of kebabs on his plate. They raised their eyebrows in surprise, but beyond that, they didn't say anything, nor did they take any active part in the conversation that evening. They were just content watching the non-stop entertainment unfold. So what if he drank huge amounts of their malt and ate most of the kebabs? The amusement he offered in return was well worth it.

But I was consumed with worry.

Thinking of his dead wife, I began to wonder if he had filed a police report about her suicide. Even if he didn't want to prejudge the issue and declare her dead before her time, he should have, at the very least, filed a missing person report. But looking at the way he was munching meat, my guess was that he had not gone anywhere near a police station. Since he had already downed six glasses of malt, I was not sure he would be in any condition to walk to a police station to file a report.

'Between the four walls of this room, I can tell you that my students are running this country.'

'Sorry?' I asked, because his slur had made it sound like 'my students are ruining this country'.

'My students are running this country,' Hari repeated, slurring 'running' again. 'And what tales they tell me! When they are with me, there is no difference at all. It is still like the old days. Till date, they behave like they did in their schooldays, as if they are all lined up before me like a bunch of boys looking up to me to guide them,' he continued.

'Why do they come to you? They are grown-ups now,' I asked, interrupting him for perhaps the first time.

He smiled indulgently and said, 'Most people don't grow up. It's too damn difficult, they just get older.'

'Oh,' I remarked disbelievingly.

'But that's the truth,' he insisted. 'They work, marry, have children, but they do not grow up. They just get older. Growing up is serious business. You should have the courage to love and lose.'

Then, he leaned forward drunkenly to whisper in my ear, 'You know, I feel for them. They are my boys. They might be running the country, but deep down, they are a bunch of fools. I know that and they know it. That is our secret. That is why they call me to Delhi every month for a dinner. They call it the guidance dinner. Only you know this secret, no one else.'

This knowledge placed a huge burden on me, as if I had been given the keys to a Masonic lodge.

Despite my growing apprehension about him and his activities, I was curious to learn what had happened to his wife. But so far, I had been hesitating. I had not yet found a delicate way of bringing up the subject. Finally, I opted for the direct approach, 'Did you find her?'

'Find who?' he asked.

This response intrigued me even more. 'What sort of a heartless person was he?' I wondered. While I was worried sick about his wife, he was thinking of some other woman.

'Remember, you came rushing out of your house when we met this morning?' I asked, obliquely hinting at his wife.

'I tried but I was late,' Hari sighed. 'She must have left.'

'Left or leapt?' I wondered.

'She must have gone back to Mussoorie,' Hari added wistfully.

I felt like throwing him out of the house. How could I entertain a scoundrel who was chasing another woman at the very moment his wife was leaping to her death? I took a big sip of my drink to calm down, but the feeling of revulsion persisted. Like the bad taste of rotten food on the tongue, it refused to go away.

'I was very keen to meet her and spend some quality time with her,' he added earnestly.

The fact that I was showing no interest in his lecherous pursuit did not seem to faze him. He was keen to complete what he had to say.

'It was a friend in Bombay who had sent her to me,' he continued.

I looked blankly at him, my regret at inviting such a man for dinner growing by the minute. Frankly speaking, I would have liked to ask him, 'Tell me, why are so interested in another woman?' But I didn't have the courage to ask.

Shiv and Shyam, too, must have wondered at my lack of judgement in inviting this man. Shiv was bound to snidely remark sometime or the other, 'Look at the company Sat keeps.' But for the moment, he was observing everything.

'She is a smart woman, this one. I was keen as hell to meet her,' Hari added in a voice loud enough to be heard from a mile away. All this while, he was thumping the table to emphasize his point and was taking larger gulps of his malt, forcing me to refill his glass frequently.

'But this idiot of a man, my driver-cum-cook,' he clarified, 'he told her, "Saheb is busy writing. He can't meet anyone."

Having shooed her away, this fool comes into the house to tell me that he has sent her off, as though he has done something great. That's why I had come out running.'

'I see.'

'This girl,' he said guiltily, 'you see, this girl is the daughter of an old friend from Bombay. We are not just friends, we are really thick. Isn't it my duty to look after his daughter when she is visiting? The least I could do was offer her lunch. But this idiotic man dispatched her like garbage.'

'And your wife?'

'What about her?' Hari questioned, knitting his eyebrows.

'Where is she?" I asked tactlessly.

This time he did not reach for his glass. Instead, colour seemed to drain from his cheeks. I could also notice a couple of drops of perspiration on his face. He shifted uncomfortably in his seat before he could speak again. 'It hurts. Even now it hurts,' he said darkly.

'Oh!' I replied, anticipating a scandal.

'But how can one fight fate?' Hari added thoughtfully.

I looked carefully at Hari, concentrating particularly on his eyes. I have always believed that eyes are the mirror into one's soul. It is easy to disguise the facial expression and hide your real feelings. But no matter how hard a person tries, it is not possible to make the eyes lie. Hari's eyes betrayed pain.

'At least she did not suffer for long,' he whispered finally.

Hari did not stay long thereafter—in fact he hardly touched his malt again. Suddenly, he was in a pensive mood, wanting to be alone.

'The strange thing with life is that in the end you are alone,' he said as he was leaving. 'If you are lucky you go quickly after your partner. But if you are unfortunate like me, you lie miserably tossing and turning in your bed wondering why she chose to go away alone. And then, you have to battle the ghosts all by yourself. The days do not bother me, I keep busy somehow. But nights are difficult to pass.'

'Nights frighten me,' Hari added weakly, as he walked out into the dark.

t e n

'There is far too much death in our lives these days,' Shiv said sombrely, as he watched the receding vision of Hari's car.

If he had added that death dominated Mussoorie, he would not have been wrong. To tell the truth, I have always associated Mussoorie with ghosts. As teenagers, we used to avoid going beyond the Library Point at night because the local rumour was that a ghost sold peanuts in a dark corner there.

If someone went there with the idea of buying peanuts roasted on slow-burning coal, the first thing he would notice would be the twisted hands of the peanut seller. Then, as the buyer would lower his eyes to avoid looking at the peanut seller, he would see his feet. They would not be like the normal feet people like you and I have. His feet would be turned backwards, as if someone had chopped them off before surgically sewing them back in a reverse position.

You can imagine the effect it could have on a person on a cold, dark, windy night. All this unfortunate buyer of peanuts would see through the mist would be a pair of disjointed hands and weirdly positioned feet. People would often hear a loud scream in the middle of the night as the frightened customer scampered away. Some people would faint right there, next to the slow-burning coal.

'There's death, and there are the Mussoorie ghosts,' Shiv said. 'I suppose they are interconnected—one follows the other.'

'That's what makes Mussoorie so interesting. There is so much variety here, among the ghosts and among the living. Even this Hari fellow is a colourful character,' I said by way of explaining my decision to invite him. 'In Delhi, we live in separate silos; there is hardly any contact with the neighbour. But Mussoorie is an open theatre, everyone knows everyone else. Sometimes I wish I could stay here forever.'

'It is time to sleep,' they both said, turning towards their rooms.

Frankly speaking, I was a little disappointed. Why did they leave abruptly when I was speaking of living here forever? Did they suspect that I was eyeing their house? I am sensitive by nature and when such a thought strikes me, I keep brooding about it endlessly. And on most nights, I end up having a severe headache.

I had expected that we would linger and talk about Mrs Keeling because this was our first night at her house. We should have remembered her for all the little things that she used to do for us and of the good times we had had with her. But they seemed to be in a hurry to get away.

They may have left abruptly, but I still had Mrs Keeling's memories for company. Had they stayed, I would have told them about the first big life lesson she had taught me. So far, I had kept it a precious secret, but that night, I would have shared it with them.

So, I sat alone and thought of that time. I had been a little over fifteen. Back then, she would listen to me attentively, indulging me and smiling all the time. One day I had said something particularly nasty about a friend. Her expression had changed suddenly. She had frozen for a moment and had looked greatly agitated. But this had lasted for only a moment; she had composed herself quickly, returning once again to her usual calm self. It was then that she had told me this little tale.

Once, a young couple moved into a new neighbourhood. Every morning, when they had breakfast, the young wife would look out of the window at their neighbour's clothes line and remark, 'Their clothes look dirty. They should use a better soap.' This went on for a month. Every morning, she would look out of the window and criticize her neighbour for her sloppy washing.

Then, one day, she looked out of the window and her eyes widened in surprise. 'Look,' she told her husband, 'they have changed the soap. The clothes look so white!'

Mrs Keeling had put her right hand softly on my shoulder, and looking gently into my eyes, she had asked, 'Can you guess what happened?'

Without waiting for me to scratch my head and say no, she had added, 'The neighbours had not changed the soap, nor had they used a special whitener on their clothes. The difference was made by the young woman's husband, in their own house. He had washed their dirty windows that morning, and through the clean windows of her home, the neighbour's clothes didn't look dirty any longer.'

Then, she had given me the great mantra of life: 'Remember always, my child, the world is as you see it. It is your attitude that shapes your world.'

It was difficult to put to practice what she said, still I carried her mantra in my heart and constantly made the effort to follow it. I should add that she gave me many gifts in her lifetime, but this was the one I cherished the most.

I would have liked to share this precious gift with Shyam and Shiv.

---

eleven

*I*t was overcast the next morning. A cold wind was blowing in from the higher hills around Mussoorie, adding a chill to the low temperature. We decided to laze around the house with mugs of tea and platefuls of hot pakoras. The funny thing about pakoras is that they are addictive; no matter how many you might have eaten, you want more. That morning, we ate piles of crisp, hot pakoras.

As we ate, we talked of old times. At one point, Shiv asked me, 'Ever since I can remember, you have wanted to settle down in Mussoorie. Haven't you ever thought of buying a place here?'

'I've tried. I told you about it.'

'Nah, you didn't.'

I felt like I had told them, but I may have been mistaken because I was getting rather forgetful. In fact, I had to constantly remind myself of the tasks for the day. Sometimes I wrote them down on a piece of paper, but then I forgot where I had kept that paper and would spend the rest of the day looking for it.

If old age had caught up with me in this respect, it had

spared Shiv marvellously. He had great memory and he was still heartbreakingly handsome. There was not a single worry line on his face, nor any grey hair on his head. His skin was flawless except for the crow's feet which appeared around the corners of his eyes when he smiled.

'No, you have not told us about this house,' Shiv repeated, and Shyam nodded in support.

'There is this group of friends I have from the civil services, bureaucrats in different departments of the government. I think you've met them.' I was reasonably sure I had introduced them.

'Have we? I doubt it,' Shiv mumbled. 'You never introduce us to your elite circle.'

I thought it was an awful remark to make to a friend you were meeting after a long time. But this was expected from Shiv because he was constantly looking for little ways to slight me. I would be lying if I said his remarks did not hurt me. But whenever Shiv said something nasty, I would think of the mantra Mrs Keeling had given me, and reinterpret his remark as simply silly.

'Did you buy a piece of land, or was it a constructed house? Let's go and see it now,' Shyam trilled enthusiastically.

Shyam was a wise man, sensitive to others' feelings. Therefore his enquiry baffled me. Why were the two of them keen to know whether or not I had acquired a house in Mussoorie?

I did not want to make an issue of it, so I said, 'Wait. Let me tell you.'

'Tell us on the way. Let's go,' Shyam insisted.

'There's nowhere to go to. It was just my fancy in overdrive,'

I told them finally.

For some weird reason, they found it funny. At first, Shiv and Shyam made an effort to look serious. But I could see that it was a losing battle. Slight smiles followed uncontrolled mirth. Within seconds, they were clutching their stomach and rolling with laughter.

Some people are miserly when they laugh, they allow just the hint of a forced smile on their lips. Others gurgle, it is difficult to make out if that silly smile on their face is a smirk or something more wholesome. I am wary of them; they are the kind of people who have things to hide.

Shiv and Shyam did not belong to that category. They laughed freely; they wanted to celebrate every happy moment of life because for them what was happening now was real. As men who were naturally generous, theirs was full-throated laughter. When they laughed in tandem, as they were doing now, it sounded like the celebratory roar of a distant thunder. Like that rumble, theirs was a harmless, infectious intimation of something good and pleasant.

Moreover, they were of a healthy English stock; that fact came through clearly in their tall bodies and generous proportions. A pair of goras laughing lustily could be infectious. So others would join in and laugh lustily. But that roar could intimidate as well.

I had known them well enough to be their second skin. I also knew that their large size and the roaring thunder of their laughter gave an illusion of menace, nothing more. Their fulfilment came from human contact and general bonhomie. A pair like that could not be threatening. Above all, they were my friends since forever.

The thing about old friends is that there are no inhibitions between them. There are no secrets between really good friends, anything and everything is easily discussed. You may be meeting after years, yet you start from where you left off. The same intimacy, that easy informality of the past takes over. Reflexively people begin to share their most intimate secrets, unburdening themselves. Friends become the sounding board for doubts and aspirations as well. Such friends are rare, but they exist.

Despite my reservations about Shiv, I could say without hesitation that Shyam and he belonged to that rare category. There was no contradiction between my bickering with Shiv and our affection.

All of a sudden, Shiv asked, 'What happened to that bird?' There was an amused twinkle in his eyes as he posed the query.

'Which bird?' I pretended to be clueless. To tell the truth, I found it offensive that Shiv had called Sati a bird.

'Give him a stiff drink and he will open up,' Shyam prompted.

'Sat is so transparent,' Shiv added.

'I see,' I said lamely, avoiding eye contact with them. 'What will they come up with now?' I wondered.

'You are so sensitive that no one has to make a great effort to read what's on your mind. You blush when you have something to hide. Your eyes crinkle and you laugh embarrassedly as if just by that you can deflect a query,' Shyam carried on, ribbing me. 'That awkward laughter is a dead giveaway.'

I shifted in my seat and laughed uncomfortably.

'See, that's typical,' Shiv sniggered, pointing towards me. 'This is precisely how he reacts.' Then, jabbing a finger in my direction, he said, 'Why are you so coy? Tell us what happened? You were in love—you were to marry her.'

'Love and marriage are not bound together like horse and carriage,' I replied. 'Love doesn't always end in marriage.'

'But you were made for each other. You were supposed to marry her,' Shiv persisted.

I might have been imagining things, but his curiosity did not seem very innocent to me.

'I was supposed to,' I whispered softly.

'What do you mean "supposed" to? That's unfair,' Shyam protested.

There were a thousand reasons why I should have married her, and not even one that suggested otherwise. Yet, we could not marry…

'It was unfair to her,' I agreed meekly.

'Unfair!' Shiv repeated, 'You mean she was just a passing phase, and then you moved on?'

I wanted to tell him that it was not so simple. Life is arranged in a complicated way and the relationships are so incomprehensible that you end up feeling bewildered. But I let it be because he would have found some other way of hurting me. Sadly, that was how it was with Shiv.

However, Shyam said helpfully, 'I remember the time when you used to say to her, "Because of you, for you and to be with you, so many ghosts pursue me all through the day. I keep thinking of you, of what I'll say to you and what we will do together when we are just by ourselves".'

'Each time she would say, "Life is no easy walk,"' I completed softly. 'Every time she would say this I would be apprehensive. I had this feeling that, one day, she would grab the memory of what we had shared and go far away.'

And thus, I began my story.

twelve

Sat

I am not a great believer in spreading misery. Therefore, after my last and unfortunate meeting with Sati, I thought it best to leave Delhi for a couple of days so I wouldn't run into people who knew us both, and who could bring up the issue of us going our separate ways. I had visions of people stopping me on the road to ask what had happened.

Some may have been genuinely concerned; they may have wanted to know why this had to happen to two really nice human beings. Others, more gossipy, would have tried to ferret out the details of that last meeting. But the worst part was the tales that some would carry, imaginative accounts of a remark I may or may not have made against Sati.

Actually, nothing out of the ordinary happened in that meeting. It was only a culmination of events that had been building up since before the meeting. At first, I was tentative. I sat down slowly, taking care to spread the tail of my coat around me. I struggled to come up with something that interested her, that would make her look up from her plate.

There were questions in my mind but I decided not to ask them because she had fallen into a strange, melancholy silence. Finally, she looked up to say, 'Happiness is temporary, sadness lingers.'

With that, she sealed our fate. The first night was the roughest. I spent it half-awake, tossing and turning in bed. After that, it became a routine for me. I continued to be restless but the repetition somewhat dulled the pain. I had already lost my parents and now the only woman I had ever loved was gone. How much more was there to lose? In this state of anxiety, I wondered if I was suited to live with any woman at all.

So, to let the dust settle, I wanted to leave the city for a few days. That's how I ended up going on a wild adventure.

Bhangarh was about three hours of a lazy drive away from Delhi. It was known as a ghost town—certified as such by the mighty government authorities. Close to Bhangarh was the game sanctuary of Sariska. I had planned to stay in a hotel in Sariska and take a day trip by bus to Bhangarh—the two together promised to provide a good mix of fangs and creeps.

I reached Sariska early morning, well before sunrise. Since the hotel and the bus stop were located in the same compound, all I needed to do was park my car, check into the hotel, and get back in time to catch the only bus that made the daily trip to Bhangarh. This was the prescribed procedure for all tourists who wished to visit Bhangarh. I had planned to follow that script, but as I was opening the boot of the car to get my bag, I had a change of heart. I decided that instead of leaving it behind in the hotel, I would take the bag with me to Bhangarh. After all, the bus could have a mechanical failure and I would perhaps need to spend the night there.

Someone else seemed to have read my thoughts. I felt a strong hand grip my right arm. 'You won't need it in the bus,' he snapped.

'Why?' I asked, my body bent over the boot as his hand continued to hold me in a vice-like grip. 'What if the bus breaks down? I may have to spend the night there.'

'No one spends a night there,' the voice intoned menacingly from behind me.

'Leave the bag in the car or in the hotel; the choice is yours. But you are not taking it along,' he added, releasing my arm.

Then he turned to leave for the bus, parked about fifty yards away. 'I leave in five minutes, with or without you,' he shouted from inside the bus. It was possible that I was seeing snakes where none existed, yet there was a no-nonsense edge to his tone. 'Thank you so much, but don't even think of arguing with me'—it was that firm an ultimatum. On the other hand, one could say that the bus driver just wanted to get on with his job, and he did not want any smart-alecky city slicker getting in his way to delay him.

'Five minutes,' he repeated, holding open his right hand, just in case I had not gotten the verbal message. Getting it all done in five minutes was no challenge. It was a simple matter of picking up my bag from the boot of the car, then ambling across to the hotel to check in, and leaving the bag with the reception, before beginning the walk back to the solitary bus at the bus stand. Yet, it worried me because of the imponderables; for instance, what if the receptionist was on a loo break?

I was getting more and more worked up as I walked towards the hotel. Therefore, my agitation knew no bounds as I stood in front of the shut door of the hotel. Hotels were expected to welcome guests with open doors, but this hotel in the middle of nowhere was a rude exception.

'Bastards,' I sneered at the shut door.

I banged my bag down on the ground and stretched my hand towards the handle of the door to push it open. But before I could grip the handle, it started to spookily turn on its own. I looked around suspiciously. From behind the door, the receptionist stepped out. 'Give me your bag. You can check-in when you return.'

It would be an understatement to say that I was overwhelmed. I kept thanking him. But he interrupted me. 'Hurry up, otherwise you will miss the bus.'

Before I turned to leave, he handed me a paper bag. 'There is a sandwich and a bottle of water in this. You will need it for the journey.'

I was still shaking my head in disbelief as I stepped into the bus. 'Good,' the driver said, looking at his watch, 'one more passenger and we are ready to go.'

The other passenger ambled in leisurely with just two seconds to spare. It was enough time for him to settle into a seat near mine. At 7 a.m. sharp, the driver turned the key in the ignition and we were on our way to Bhangarh. But my attention remained focused on the other passenger.

Was it on purpose that he had boarded the bus with just seconds to spare? Why had he chosen a seat close to mine when the entire bus was empty?

He was wearing the traditional Rajasthani dress—a turban, a short kurta and a tied-between-the-legs dhoti. The dress was quaint, but that was what men in those parts had been wearing since forever. However, what struck me as most odd was the colour of his turban. It was not the usual red colour; his was a mourning black. The rest of his dress was dirty pale, an originally white-coloured cloth that must have turned pale after years of use. His physical appearance, too, was odd. He was a tall, ruggedly built man with a skin colour that matched the pale colour of his clothes. His skin was wrinkled. But it was his eyes that gripped my attention. It would be wrong to call them eyes because they were nothing like normal eyes.

The eyes, or what should have been eyes, were actually two black sockets from which regular eyes had been jacked out. It seemed as if someone had viciously scooped them out, the same way in which we scoop ice cream from a tub. Something else about our bus journey struck me as odd. The driver had been unsparing with me, adopting a no-nonsense attitude right from the beginning. Like a rigid schoolmaster, he had wanted compliance from me. And he had pointedly looked at his watch when I had boarded the bus.

But when this other man had gotten into the bus a mere

two seconds before seven, the driver had said nothing, nor had he given him the look. In fact, he had studiously avoided that man's gaze. They hadn't even exchanged greetings, nor had he nodded his head in acknowledgement of the man's presence. Yet, they seemed to know each other intimately.

'I am Sat,' I tried to make conversation with my fellow passenger. Hearing this, the driver pressed hard on the accelerator pedal and the bus raced ahead in response, throwing us back against our seats. I grunted angrily and expected my fellow traveller to say something. But he had closed his eyes, dropping his eyelids like shutters over those dark holes.

Then, I noticed his hands. They were not ordinary hands—the short and stubby fingers of both his hands were bent backwards. Those hands could not be put to any functional use.

'Was he the peanut-selling ghost of the Library Point in Mussoorie or his local clone?' I wondered uneasily. Whoever, or whatever it was, it had begun to scare the daylights out of me.

I was afraid. I was sweating and very worried that I would die prematurely; my life had been insignificant so far and now my death would remain common. I had truly gotten myself into a terrible mess; the bus driver looked like a dubious character and my co-passenger was definitely a ghost. Together, they made an evil pair.

Now that I was assessing the matter critically, even the hotel receptionist's eagerness to hurry me along on to this trip appeared suspicious. Why had he been so anxious to send me away? 'He, too, must belong to their gang,' I thought. When weird thoughts like this begin to spin in my mind, there is no stopping them.

Finally, I decided that I had to distract myself, otherwise I would become a nervous wreck if I kept worrying about who they were and what their intentions were. So, I turned my face towards the window to avoid looking at my fellow traveller. The view out of the window was reassuring. The bleak, barren plains of Sariska were slowly giving way to green bushes and trees. But how long could a person keep his neck twisted at a right angle to the body? Moreover, this continuous parade of scenery whizzing past created a feeling of nausea, so willy-nilly, I had to turn my face away from the window.

'How much time to Bhangarh?' I shouted to the bus driver.

'Two hours, maybe more. You never know in these parts. Try to get some sleep, you will need the energy in Bhangarh.'

There was no way I was going to be caught off guard by these two, so I decided to do all I could to prevent myself from falling asleep. Once again, I resumed my vigil by the window. This time, I squiggled to turn my body sideways for comfort and pressed my face against the glass to feel its coolness against my cheek. The increasingly thick foliage outside was diverting in its variety; soothed by it, I let my restless mind wander again.

Undoubtedly, I had wanted to get away from the real world for a while, but was it only adventure that had brought me here? Or was there a desire to be consumed by the supernatural? There were numerous mysterious accounts about Bhangarh and all of them maintained that it was unlike any other town in Rajasthan. In the past, it had been a bustling place. Its reputation for sorcery was its claim to fame in Rajasthan. Almost every household in this town had specialized in one magic trick or the other.

Chura Singh, the greatest magician of all times, had belonged to this town. People still say in hushed tones that he was a true master of magic. Everything about him was in superlatives. He was a great magician, a super sorcerer and a man with a huge libido; he was also a real rascal who did not mind using his powers deviously. No one knew which time and age he lived in, but the general guess was that he had existed around five or six centuries ago.

Among his most famous acts of magic was the ability to disappear. He would utter the 'lauki mantra', close his eyes, and that was it. One moment you would see him and the next he would not be there. People would rub their eyes in disbelief and wonder how a phenomenon like that could take place right in front of their eyes—that a man of flesh, bones and blood could vanish.

He had many other tricks up his sleeve. For example, he had mastered the 'sher bandh mantra'. He would chant it to a tiger in a remarkably melodious voice as if he was making love to the creature. By doing so five times, he would sedate an angry tiger.

Once it so happened that a tiger from Sariska strayed into Bhangarh and walked right up to the central square of the town. It was a pleasant Sunday afternoon when men, women and children were thronging the market in great numbers. The fact that the Diwali festival was just round the corner was another reason for the larger-than-usual turnout of people.

The tiger had no means of knowing the difference between

a holiday crowd and an ordinary day's sparse number. Nor did he have any idea of what a market was. So, he ambled along merrily till he found himself in the middle of a vast crowd.

People were busy shopping, so they did not notice the beast at first. After a while, a group of small children saw it, and they tried to grab its tail, mistaking it for an overgrown cat. It was only then, when he found himself surrounded by irritating kids, that he panicked and let out a roar. Hearing the ear-splitting roar, everyone froze. A moment later, panic set in and screaming children shuffled to get behind the protective folds of their parents' garments. A few old women fainted at the sight of the animal. But some of the younger men saw it as an opportunity to impress young women. They crouched in a circle around the tiger to take him on, secretly hoping that the need would not arise.

A lone police officer was on festival duty at the square. Instead of doing his job, he was taking a siesta outside a tea shop. Even the roar of the tiger failed to wake him up. But when the crowd began to stir, and an old woman shrieked before fainting, he sensed something was very wrong, that his job could be at stake. He roused himself slowly and even before he was fully awake, he waved his baton in the air to habitually shout, 'Halt!'

The police officer's command made the tiger suspicious. He looked around warily and let out another ear-splitting roar. By now, the tiger was crouching on the ground, ready to pounce on whoever threatened him. Anything could have happened then, and in that confusion, the tiger could have mauled people. At that critical juncture, Chura Singh materialized out of thin air.

There was hope now. People shuffled hurriedly to make way and Chura Singh walked regally through this passage to stop just a few feet short of the curious tiger.

He looked at the tiger in the eye and began to chant the 'sher bandh mantra' sonorously. By the time he had finished the third chant, the tiger had begun purring like a cat. At the end of the fifth chant, the tiger walked slowly towards Chura Singh and lay down at his feet in total surrender. Chura Singh was already a celebrity in Bhangarh, but after taming the tiger in front of everyone, his reputation began to spread far beyond the borders of the state. Even this was nothing in comparison to the glory that was yet to come.

Sometime after the incident with the tiger, Bhangarh suffered a severe draught. By the end of the second year, the stocks of grain of the kingdom had reduced to a dangerous level. The grazing ground for the animals turned brown, there was not a blade of grass for miles around. As a result, animals started dying in hordes and people were falling by the dozen.

Since the scorching sun did not hold out any hope of relief, people of Bhangarh gathered in front of Chura Singh's house. He was busy stirring bubbling cauldrons with mysterious herbs when he heard the commotion and the cries for help. It was then that he cast his most potent spell. Within minutes, the skies darkened, and even as people were standing outside his house, it began to rain.

It may have been pure coincidence that it rained after he chanted his hocus-pocus, but people thought it was his magical powers which had moved the Rain God. This ability to tame nature established him as the second-most powerful person in the state, after the king. So, in gratitude, people built a grand octagonal palace for him on top of a hill overlooking the town. All this adulation went to Chura Singh's head. With a bloated head, he began to believe that he was equal to the king, if not the gods themselves. Around this time, he fell hopelessly in love with the young princess of Bhangarh. As is often the case with people in desperate but one-sided love, he began to dwell in a state of romantic illusion.

As a practising illusionist of the highest order, he knew he was letting himself get sucked deeper and deeper into a crisis. But he was beyond care; his passion outstripped common sense. It was no longer possible for him to control his fantasies.

Our bus had reached the outskirts of Bhangarh. I could already see the distant outlines of a palace and a great temple. A little beyond, and towering over them, the shape of an impressive octagonal structure was also visible. As we drove closer to the town, I could see rows of neatly laid out houses separated by wide avenues. We must have been a mere kilometre away from Bhangarh when I saw a sign by the roadside, warning, 'Entering the borders of Bhangarh after sunset is strictly prohibited.' The word 'strictly' was painted in bold letters.

'Why?' I whispered to myself. 'Why must people leave before sunset?'

The man sitting across me heard me muttering because he opened his eyes. For a moment, I had the impression that I could see a film of wetness in the hollow of his eyes. But he turned his face away abruptly.

At last the bus reached Bhangarh. It stopped in what must have been a field or a horse-racing arena once. 'Bhangarh!' the driver shouted to us informatively, waiting for us to get down. I bent down to tie my shoelaces. It must have taken me no more than twenty seconds, but by the time I got up, my fellow passenger had vanished into thin air, leaving the bus door ajar behind him.

'Welcome to the land of magic,' I thought to myself. Meanwhile, the driver, who had gotten down from the front end of the bus, was limbering up on the ground. 'Where are you going?' I asked.

'Wherever you are going,' he snapped, jabbing a finger at me, 'we have two hours here. At 12:00 sharp, we shoot like an arrow for Sariska to have lunch there.'

'Can't we eat here? There is a lot of time to sunset.'

'Where will you eat? Do you see any people? There are no restaurants here, not even a tea shop,' he replied firmly. 'There is no time to waste, let's go.' He grabbed my hand, leaving me no scope to linger.

'No time to waste' seemed to be his favourite phrase. Every few minutes, he would fling it at me to end an argument. I would try to start a discussion, the most essential conversation really, and he would say, 'No time to waste.'

'What's the hurry?' I persisted.

'No time to waste,' he repeated, dragging me along.

The bus had stopped at the edge of the town. Now we were heading towards its centre. I could see a high wall in the distance, running along the boundary of the town.

'Tall and wide,' the driver hummed as he saw me looking at the wall, 'thirty feet high and five feet wide. There are two walls actually; the inner one is slightly smaller and a little less wide. Together, they were impregnable. No one could breach them.'

But all of a sudden, the lilt went out of his voice, as if someone had tampered with the tone control switch, and he snapped again, 'No time to waste.'

Bhangarh was pleasing to the eye, a marvel of architecture. The neat separation of the business part of town from the residential and the recreational areas could serve as a model for any modern-day town planner.

It was eerily odd as well. The closer I got to the middle of the town, the more I was able to see those peculiar aspects; for instance, the houses were without a roof. The walls were intact. The wooden doors looked solid, but the top was missing. If you looked up from inside the house, you were in direct communion with the gods above.

It must have been a very religious town because temples proliferated and every shop had a place for an idol. Another remarkable feature of Bhangarh was the fragrance in the air; it carried the mixed smell of jasmine and lavender which were planted everywhere in the town. Despite the passage of time, these plants had survived the heat and dust of history.

When we reached the farthest end of the town, the driver pointed at a house with dancing women painted on its walls. 'This was the court dancer's haveli,' he said.

'How do you know?' I asked, not believing him completely.

'Do you see that boulder?' he asked, pointing towards a big

piece lying close to the principal entrance of the house. 'There were no house numbers then. People, especially important people, announced their presence by having distinctive symbols, like those dancing figures, carved into the boulder. In this case, the court dancer also had them painted on the outer walls of the house, just to make sure.'

Suddenly, the driver became anxious. 'Let's go back,' he hissed.

We began to walk back at a much faster pace towards the bus.

'Tell me, why do they have that sign warning visitors not to stay beyond sunset?' I asked breathlessly.

'Bhangarh was known for its black magic.'

'Magic or black magic?' I interrupted.

'It was known for both, but it was famous for black magic. A man called Chura Singh was the greatest magician of them all.'

'He could tame tigers, and disappear into magician thin air?' I asked.

'It was the very same man,' the driver confirmed. 'Do you know he fell desperately in love with a princess called Ratnawati?'

I nodded. I had heard a part of the story. But it sounded quite fantastical and I wasn't sure if it was a fact or an embroidered version of someone's overactive imagination.

'Right from the beginning, Chura Singh knew that he had trapped himself into an impossible tangle. Leave aside the impossibility of reciprocation by the princess, there was no real chance that he would even be able to get anywhere near her. But after taming the tiger, and after all the adulation of the town people, he thought he had become an equal of sorts to the royal family. Moreover, love makes people do weird things.

'One day he was walking around in the marketplace. It was probably somewhere here, right around the spot we are standing on just now. By chance, he noticed the princess's maid buying hair oil from a market stall. Chura Singh thought it was his great opportunity. So, he lingered around the oil-seller's stall and cast a spell on the oil. It was an all-powerful spell, even the most potent antidote known to man could not neutralize it.'

'Then what happened?' I asked impatiently.

'The maid was a simpleton. She saw Chura Singh bending over the urn but did not suspect that magic might work on oil.' The driver continued, 'She paid for the oil, and in a most courtly manner, she thanked the shopkeeper before returning merrily to the palace with the urn of oil.'

'The princess was intelligent, well-versed in worldly affairs, and she had a very observant eye. She immediately noticed the swirling oil in the urn. "This means trouble," she thought to herself. Princess Ratnawati knew a bit of magic herself. She knew that if she touched the oil even slightly, the spell on it would ensure that she would have to surrender herself to the magician.

'So, she threw the urn away with all her strength. The urn landed on a big stone and the oil spilled on the rock. Drenched fully in oil, the stone began to roll forward. By the time it reached the marketplace, where the magician was standing in anticipation of the princess, the stone had gathered great speed. Since the magician had cast a supreme spell on the oil, this oil-soaked stone had to reach the object of its desire. It hit the magician at great speed, causing instant death.

'Before dying, the villainous magician put a curse on his own town. Everyone, he declared, would die within a week of his own death. No one would be reborn, neither here nor anywhere else. Bhangarh would remain a ghost town forever.'

'Oh!' I sighed.

'That's not all. Remember, the princess herself was somewhat of an expert in occult science? She cast a spell in return. She told the town people that while she could not neutralize the curse of that devilish magician and though they would never be reborn in flesh and blood because of it, their spirits would be free to roam forever. They would be able to return every night to Bhangarh.'

'Oh!'

'As Chura Singh had predicted, everyone in Bhangarh died within a week. Since that day this town comes alive every night, just as the princess had predicted.' The driver added cheerfully, 'Soon after the sun sets, bazaars begin to hum with activity. Women in all their finery throng the stalls filled with the finest silk and jewellery. People wear clothes which are latest in fashion; there is dance and general merriment till dawn. But before the first rays of sun hit the town, it returns to its deserted look. Bhangarh becomes dead again in the morning, as if the night was a mirage—an elaborate but unreal charade.'

'Oh!' I whispered distractedly a third time. 'But how do you know what happens at night? After all, no living being can enter the town after sunset.'

'Good question.' The driver patted me on the back encouragingly, simultaneously nudging me to get into the bus.

RAJIV DOGRA

This time, I was in a hurry to leave Bhangarh. 'Let's go,' I urged as soon as I got into my seat.

I began to breathe normally only after we had passed the sign saying, 'Entering the borders of Bhangarh after sunset is strictly prohibited.'

'Where is he?' I asked, suddenly realizing that I was the only passenger in the bus.

'He never comes back,' the driver responded casually, without bothering to look back.

'Never comes back?' I echoed with a tremor in my voice. 'But you said no one stays in Bhangarh after sunset.' I was gripping the back of the seat in front of me tightly, and my knuckles had turned white with the effort.

'Yes, he never comes back,' the driver repeated, pressing the accelerator pedal.

Just like the previous occasion, this time too I was thrown back on my seat. I had the feeling that these strategically timed accelerations of the bus were deliberate. They were the driver's responses to tricky questions.

Suddenly I felt the air inside the bus turn cold. A sharp, warm breath caressed my neck and I thought I heard someone say, 'I alone can come back from the dead.'

'Oh!' I parroted, and turned around quickly. But I couldn't see anyone behind me. I started sweating. But I sat absolutely still in my seat, afraid that the slightest movement could provoke the ghost.

'Do not think that I have gone,' someone whispered into my ears.

I stayed absolutely still, but I could feel goosebumps all over my body.

'How can I go if I pine for her?' the voice continued eerily. 'I will remain here as long as she comes to Bhangarh. Every night, I stand guard to see that no one disturbs her.'

I was expecting him to say something more; perhaps there was a story that he wanted to tell, but had not found the right listener over the centuries. But nothing followed.

The bus was quiet once more, except for the steady drone of the engine and occasional bumps over the uneven road. The air around me became tepid, and the electric tension gradually eased. But I had goosebumps for a long time. I was afraid that the cold breath and the whispering voice might return. Due to that fear, I did not turn back to see who or what might be lurking behind me.

'Relax, he has gone,' the driver said, turning back for the first time since we had left Bhangarh.

'Who was he?'

Once again, the driver accelerated in response.

When we reached Sariska, I tried one more time. 'Where is he?'

'Who?' the driver asked busily.

'That man who went with us in the morning. If he spends the night in Bhangarh, will he be alive tomorrow morning?'

'If he is alive in the first place,' the driver smiled mysteriously.

He began to walk away but I held him back and asked, 'Aren't you worried about him?'

'Why?'

'He may die. That's why.'

'I don't worry about him,' the driver responded sternly.

'But that warning on the signboard said that entering the borders after sunset was prohibited. You should have brought him back,' I persisted irritatingly.

The driver looked at me and said in a firm voice, 'He never comes back'.

'What's his name?' I asked the driver who had begun to walk away from me.

He stopped ten feet away from me and turned around. Then, very slowly, he told me the name of the other passenger.

'Chura Singh.'

$\mathscr{A}$ fierce wind blew, whisking away our tablecloth. Its sudden swirl broke the spell that my story had cast on Shiv and Shyam. They looked up as if to ask where we were.

Actually, we were busy wandering and wondering in different worlds. They were lost in the mysteries of Bhangarh. However, I was not sure if, beyond a temporary diversion, that adventure had achieved much for me.

'That was some ghost story!' Shiv intoned in the first non-caustic comment of the night. 'I wonder if that bit about people not being allowed to stay the night in Bhangarh is actually correct.'

'That's what the official signboard says,' I confirmed. 'People say that no one has dared to do that in years. Once, many, many years ago, someone had foolishly stayed there after sunset. No one heard from him again.'

'That last bit you told us about Chura Singh gave me the creeps,' Shiv admitted. 'That weird bus driver—was he real?'

'I don't know,' I replied.

I confess that the Bhangarh episode had shaken me up thoroughly. I was still not sure if that driver was actually made of flesh and blood. If he indeed was a living person, then he was brave to drive regularly with a ghost as his passenger. On the other hand, if the driver was also a ghost, then I was lucky to have escaped alive.

Then, out of the blue, Shiv asked, 'Why are songs of love so sad?'

It puzzled me that he should have asked such a question when we were on a different track. What was he alluding to? Was it something to do with the fact that I kept playing the songs Sati used to like? As a matter of fact, Shiv knew all the songs that Sati liked and I had often heard him humming them with his eyes closed. When he hummed one of her favourites, he made it sound very sensuous, as if he was fondling the notes.

I must admit, it always left me feeling suspicious. Why, with all his girls, was he interested in Sati? For a man like him, no relationship was sacred.

'Are you people still in love?' Shiv asked next.

I wondered why he was keen on finding that out. 'Yes we are,' I responded. 'Even after 35 years, we glow when we meet. It shows on our faces.'

'What about you guys?' I asked, just to keep Shiv from probing me further. 'What does love mean to you?'

'I don't know,' Shyam said blandly, but Shiv kept smiling slyly.

'Forget us and all these theories about love, tell us what happened to you guys,' Shyam added, urging me to go on.

I hesitated. I had been at the point of carrying on, but that sudden rush of wind had stopped me. It had made me cautious.

'Did you have a fall out for some reason? Was it a lovers' quarrel?' Shyam turned to look at me. To my surprise, his eyes were moist. 'I mean, you guys were genuinely in love.'

'Another girl, maybe?' Shiv interjected, winking.

'Don't be silly,' Shyam said sternly. 'Sat-Sati were truly one.'

I had not pursued distractions, at least not anything that could be called serious. I believed truly that by keeping my focus on her, my love would be more persuasive. The unvarnished truth was that I was besotted with Sati to the point of irrationality.

I was envious of the sun that touched her. Her presence made me turn weak in the knees. Her absence weakened my heart; I would become restless. Where then was the scope to think of someone else? That possibility simply did not interest me, it would have soiled a sacred relationship.

But the sanctity of relationships was never Shiv's strong point. And I had learned over the years that arguing with Shiv over a point of morality was pointless.

Shiv spun words for their tonal effect, often their essence meant nothing at all. In that sense, he was an ideal dinner companion—happy and downright gregarious. Even his silences added a touch of mystery about what might follow. Perhaps these mysterious pauses and his good manners made him irresistible to women.

When you were invited to a party with him, he was polite to a fault and constantly attentive to your slightest need. If he found you standing alone in a corner, he would rush up to you and entreat, 'Please sit down.' Then, for the next ten minutes, he would regale you with the most amusing anecdotes until he felt that you had loosened up enough to mingle with the other guests.

One day, when we were in college, I heard him tell Sati, 'I was too young to have read Dante then.'

My ears perked up. I sensed instinctively that the conversation would lead to something interesting because Shiv was not the type to talk about Dante without a purpose. He would drop big names to impress women. So, instead of moving on to join a group of friends as I had planned earlier, I decided to stay near Shiv—not too close, but behind him—like an unobtrusive fly on the wall.

'Dante had written about a woman too young to love,' Shiv continued. 'My point is very simple; how can a third person decide what is the right age for someone to fall in love? Love strikes whimsically; even a child can fall in love. It hardly matters then whether you are female or male. Both can be equally silly in love. I will tell you about my first love.'

'Tell me,' Sati trilled, interested.

'The first stirrings of love stay with you forever. It is the most precious…' For once Shiv was lost for words. He fumbled a bit before he found his bearing, 'It is like your first bike, your first salary and your very first bank account.'

Sati was listening to him attentively, but his comparison of love with material things confused her. Her expression changed from curious interest to deep enquiry.

That did not trouble Shiv. He always took pride in saying

that he was capable of holding his own on any subject. To sum it up, Shiv was didactic—a rigid fundamentalist in the validity of his ideas.

'If I am paying for the meal then I have the right to lecture,' he would often assert.

Once, someone had asked him bluntly why he did not let others speak. Shiv had retorted that it was a strange question to ask. In a democracy, everyone had an equal right to speak. How could he, Shiv, force anyone to speak if they did not want to speak?

Then, turning his venom against the questioner, he had said, 'The problem with you is that you ask too many questions.'

Before the questioner could have recovered, Shiv had delivered the punchline. 'I have a fundamental objection to your statement. If I let others speak, it would mean that I should stay silent. Isn't that the logical conclusion?'

'Yes, you have a point there.'

'That would be absolutely unacceptable to me. I had learned very early in my life that silence is another way of telling a lie,' Shiv had continued. 'As you should know very well by now, I would rather die than tell a lie. So please don't ask me to stay silent.'

'You are right,' the questioner had responded meekly. He had also been in a hurry to finish his meal.

That was how he was with men—brusque and domineering. But a woman like Sati was different. Shiv was attentive to a fault and careful with his words. That was why Shiv was quick to sense that Sati's interest in their conversation had reduced.

Returning quickly to the theme he had started with, Shiv began again, 'I was telling you about the first time. I think I was about twelve at that time, but mind you, a grown-up twelve-year-old who knew that boys and girls could play games other than sports. One day, in the middle of the school term, we had a new teacher. It was quite normal for a teacher to leave for another job and to have her place filled up immediately by someone new. No one took much notice of the switch because it was usually the case of one harassed middle-aged teacher replacing another disgruntled person. But this new teacher was a class apart.'

'Very interesting,' Sati said coquettishly.

'She was so pretty that not one of us twenty adolescent boys could concentrate on the blackboard. Even the girls in our class worshipped the very ground she walked on. Speaking of my own condition, I must admit that I was entranced from the moment she stepped into our class.'

'Entranced or enchanted?' Sati asked.

'Entranced, my dear Sati, entranced,' Shiv insisted. 'She must have noticed my intense look because sometimes I got the impression that she was reciprocating my interest. I cannot vouch for it but there were definitely moments when she paid more attention to me than to the other students in our class. Before this new teacher came into our class, I used to rush home after school to quickly change and play cricket with my friends. But where was the time now?'

Sati smiled, thinking of a 12-year-old infatuated with a teacher twice his age. But then, she had also heard of the French President Macron, who, as a teenager, had pursued his teacher and later married her. Viewed in that light, Shiv's story did not seem unusual.

'Ever since this teacher came into my life, I could only think of her,' Shiv carried on. 'So much so that one afternoon my grandmother came up to me, and ruffling my hair, she said, "I think you are in love."

'Granny was the wise one in the family. If she said something, the rest of us listened. There was no room for counter-questions. When she reached a conclusion, we deferred to her. So, if she said I was in love, then I had to be in love. It was in the beginning of spring when Granny had concluded that I was in love. Sometime soon after that, our class was taken out for a picnic to a large park outside the city.

'I still remember every little detail of that day. The weather was perfect, neither too sunny nor too warm. A pleasant breeze kept blowing in the park throughout the time that we were there. In short, it was an ideal day for young lovers. We were about to finish our lunch when the teacher started singing. It was a song of love and longing—Bhanwara Bada Naadan...'

'How romantic!' Sati chirped.

'If you were to ask me why she chose that particular song, I wouldn't have an answer,' Shiv continued. 'I have thought about it constantly, but even after all these years, it remains a beautiful puzzle. However, I recall clearly that her eyes kept darting back to me throughout the time that she sang.'

'And you thought she too was in love,' Sati said in jest.

Shiv nodded shyly.

'Later, at home, I must have sung that song a hundred times.

And every single time, I would focus on her picture in the class portrait that hung over my desk. The morning after the picnic, I went to school with a spring in my step.'

'Then what happened?' Sati asked.

'That day, I mean on the day following the picnic, a man came to meet her in school. She brought him into our class just before the final bell. And by way of an introduction, she said simply, "Class, meet my husband."'

'Oh,' Sati mumbled politely, 'you must have been shocked.'

'To say that I was shocked would be an understatement. For the first time in my life, I felt the world collapse around me. "Was life worth living any longer?" I wondered. Her announcement made me sweat so much that there were huge wet patches of sweat under my armpits. Blood had rushed up to colour my face crimson. The girl sitting next to me asked anxiously, "Do you have a fever, Shiv?" She was right in thinking that way, because I did have some sort of a fever.

'After school, I raced ahead of the others to fall in step with my teacher. The man she had brought with her to our class was also there, walking jauntily with her. I was short of breath and my face was flushed red. Even as I strained to keep pace with their longer strides, I kept looking through the corner of my eye at my rival.

'As a fully grown man, he was much taller than me. I admit that he was handsome in a rugged way, with a square jaw and a muscle-toned body. He probably had a good job too, judging by the style of his clothes. But, beyond that, there was nothing much to distinguish between us, and in my state of envy, I couldn't bring myself to call him my teacher's husband. So, I pointed towards him and asked, "Is he more handsome than me?"

'She stopped, and he stopped too. This scared me a bit, but she bent down quickly to kiss me on the forehead. Then, she turned her face up to look coquettishly towards her husband, and they sort of danced away from me.'

'That was cute,' Sati remarked.

'One learns quickly when one is young. After meeting my teacher's husband, I matured fast in matters of love.'

'What happened then?'

'Soon I fell in love again,' Shiv declared. 'This time it was a girl my age.'

'You are absolutely right,' Sati nodded. 'Young love is tempestuous. It is confused and people often find their attention slipping.'

'That is why youth opts for transience, impulsively and as a matter of expedience.'

'Did that first loss affect you deeply?'

'No, I don't think so. Not really,' Shiv responded a bit too quickly, 'but that dream died young.'

Then he scratched his head as if he was searching for inspiration. Having found it, he added, 'That first experience hardened me. I became cynical in matters of love.'

Back at my position as a fly on the wall, I kept rolling that last statement of his repeatedly in my mind. Why had he said that? Was it to gain Sati's sympathy?

fourteen

---

*T*his had happened when we had been teenagers in college. I still remember being uneasy about it because Sati would hang on to every word Shiv uttered. I often wondered why.

Sitting in Mussoorie with Shyam and Shiv, I came back to the real world and said, 'Remember, that was the year when students went on a flash strike just before the summer vacations. It was a protest against the poor quality of food, but there was some violence too. Some of the kitchen staff were beaten up by the students. I was not even aware that a strike was being observed. But as it often happens on such occasions, the ring leaders who had organized the violence ran away before the police arrived.'

'The leaders usually escape the law, it is the innocent who get caught.'

'That's exactly what happened. I had stepped out of my hostel room to go to the canteen for a cup of tea,' I said, carrying on. 'It was terrible timing on my part because the police marched in just then to round up the leaders of the protest. The leaders had vanished from the hostel, but they found me conveniently present on the scene. Moreover, I must have looked sinister to the police because I had an overgrown beard and I was marching purposefully towards the canteen. They didn't waste time to confirm if I was actually one of those who had beaten up the kitchen staff. They needed to catch someone to satisfy their bosses, so they grabbed me and took me away to the police station.

'A long weekend followed which meant that I could not be produced before a magistrate during that period. By the time my case came up for hearing, and the magistrate gave his judgement, I ended up spending a full ten days in the police lockup. I was miserable there with the common criminals, but that didn't worry me much. What bothered me was the lack of contact with Sati.'

'You were free after ten days.'

'Those ten long days changed my life,' I nodded. 'Sati left for her home in Pune. I flew out of India because my application to a college in New York had come through.'

'I don't believe this. You left without meeting her?' Shiv shouted. 'You could have telephoned her. You could have told us.'

It was normal for Shiv to react like a volcano, huffing words and puffing venom. But this was the first time I had seen him so agitated.

'In all these years you never told us,' Shiv kept haranguing me. 'Neither about your cheap trick with her, nor about sneaking off.'

'I went to New York without trying to meet her,' I corrected. 'My sense of shame made me slink away.'

'You didn't actually do that?' Shyam shouted at me.

I had done precisely that because I was a coward. Sati was morally so correct that I was worried about her reaction. How could I explain why I, among all the students, had been singled out by the police? I thought, by the time I would come back after one year, she would forgive me for the jail term I was not guilty for.

'One makes mistakes,' I told Shyam.

'You came back after a year. Did you try to meet her then?'

'I went to Pune to meet her. But she had left the city.'

'You met her family there?'

'No,' I said simply.

Sharing secrets with friends and letting go may be therapeutic, but it can also be awkward. Like shedding clothes, the embarrassment comes at the end. That was exactly what was happening to me now.

I was feeling emotionally drained and restless, like a scrap of paper fluttering about in the wind. Sensing my mood, Shiv pretended to be lost in his own world. Shyam mumbled under his breath and went into the house to look for something he did not need. I began to look around, shifting my gaze slowly from the garden to the structure of the house.

The Keeling bungalow had been built in the classic colonial style with a sloping slate roof. The roof was red in colour, in contrast to the green all round. The far end of the roof extended about two metres over the house to provide shade, and to form a protected sitting area in the event of rain. We were sitting in the veranda overlooking the valley.

The bungalow had seen better days, though it was not badly off even now. The overall ambience continued to be cheerful; there was a dash of colour about the house—every painting was festive, each landscape reflected Mrs Keeling's sunny optimism. The furniture, carefully chosen over the years, had been polished regularly. The linen in the house spelt class, and the servants were efficient and polite to a fault. A visitor to her house long remembered that stay, be it for five minutes or for five days. Mrs Keeling made sure that a guest was well looked after.

Shiv and Shyam had inherited her grace, maybe not in its entirety, but to a substantial extent. Take, for example, my case. I was like a member of the family; still they were constantly fussing over me. Was I warm enough? Did I have the right blanket? Why did I have so little food on my plate? Small things like that may be insignificant, but they are details that people remember. Yet, at that point, we were sombre, unable to find a way out of our awkwardness.

Just then I saw a thick cluster of clouds making their way towards us. Their approach gave me the courage to speak again. 'Sati had a very small family, just her parents. From what I could gather from her neighbours, her parents died within a few weeks of our finishing college. She stayed on in Pune for a few more months to settle matters. Then, she sold the house and moved away. She told her neighbours that she was going somewhere in the hills where no one would ever find her.'

'Oh!'

'I went back to New York to finish my studies. After that, I got a job and stayed there for a few more years. In fact, I left the US just before Shiv reached there.'

'Well,' Shiv said, largely for the sake of saying something. But I understood the unasked question.

'No, there was no one there,' I said.

'But still,' Shiv persisted.

'One loves only once in life,' I replied to a dedicated philanderer.

'Love multiplies when you distribute it,' Shiv joked.

'I was committed to Sati and I continued to live in hope. That hope kept me going. Plus, there was her scent.'

'Her scent?' Shyam asked.

'Yes, her scent,' I replied ponderously. 'Sati's sense, her presence, her being, her persona, whatever you call it, pursued me to New York. It was all-pervasive.'

'Life is arranged in such a complicated way,' Shyam sighed.

'She followed me to work. I would find her watching over my shoulders in official meetings, whispering encouragement. When I would pound away at the computer, I would feel her bending over me to see if I was typing correctly. Her breath would brush past my cheeks. I would smell her perfume and the scent of jasmine in her hair.'

'What about her? How did she take it?' Shiv asked. He spoilt the effect by adding, 'I wish we had known. Things may have been different.'

I should have anticipated that punchline. After all, Shiv was clever with words.

■

I had never wished ill for Shiv, not even in our most bitter moments. In fact, I felt that he would have achieved greater heights had it not been for his stubborn pride. People who met him for the first time were put off by his superior attitude. Even when he pretended to be listening to others, indifference showed on his face—as if he was telling them they were not clever enough. That was annoying, but even more upsetting was his penchant for the most bizarre statements.

'People can drown in the sky,' Shiv declared, suddenly.

'Really?' I asked.

'Grief is overwhelming. It cuts you down, making you do weird things like gazing endlessly at the sky.'

'And when you are happy?'

'When I am happy, I want to walk down the mall road to roar like a cloud.'

'Why?' Shyam asked curiously.

'Why what?' Shiv snapped.

'You want to roar because you want to make a noise or do you have a purpose in mind? Roaring clouds are an announcement of the rain. What will you do after you have spoilt everyone's peace on the mall road? What will follow your roar?'

Shiv had not thought this through, but he was not one to be trapped easily. He got up from his chair, stretched himself up to his full six-feet-plus height and raised both his arms. 'Why must everything in life have a purpose?' Shiv responded, jabbing a threatening finger at Shyam, 'Why can't we do things for our own sake? A roar is a roar, that's it.'

'You mean it is possible to be seduced by illusion,' Shyam

said quickly, 'like the search for a guru?'

'Yes, like the search for a guru,' Shiv repeated. 'Dana was foolish.'

'Foolish?' Shyam repeated, just to be sure.

'Not foolish. Let's say she was extraordinary in an ordinary way.'

'But how does that concern us?'

'It does, because you two keep ribbing me for no reason at all.' Then, without our prompting, he told us the story of Dana, the American girl.

fifteen

Shiv

They had met at a moment in life when Shiv needed space and time to reflect, and she was a drifter, seeking salvation. So, Dana was the doctor's recommendation for Shiv because she believed that melancholy was beautiful for the soul.

But after a while, she got bored with their relationship and decided to visit India. Before leaving, she met a swami in the US. By blending his nasal twang and American slang with quotations from Hindu scriptures, the swami had adapted to the American taste—easy and instant like McDonald's.

When she asked him for some quick tips for spotting a real guru, he said unabashedly, 'Give me my fees first.'

'Swami ji, I am a humble seeker,' Dana admitted after giving him the money, 'what should I look for when I reach India?'

'Seek a guru. That is the first step. Then, if you think you have found him, look into his eyes. If you look at the pictures of great sages, you will notice the faraway, otherworldly look in them. It is this look that you must find in your guru.'

'What else should I look for, Swami ji?' Dana continued.

'Observe his body language. See carefully the confidence of his movement and the way he moves his hands. It should reflect steadiness, and his body must be erect. A bent body rears a bent mind, my child,' the swami intoned.

All this while, the swami's eyes lingered over Dana's body.

'Ripe,' he thought, 'ripe like a restless young filly.' But he shook his head vigorously to look away from temptation. He was already battling a charge of molestation in an American court; he did not want another legal headache to come in the way of his green card.

'Swami ji,' Dana prompted, because all of a sudden, the swami had gotten silent.

'Remember also,' the swami said, continuing seamlessly, 'that when a great guru is asked a question, his response is preceded by a long period of silence.'

'Why this long period of silence, Swami ji? What does this silence mean?'

'Silence is the language of mystics,' the Indian swami in the US remarked gravely. 'Silence is interrupted by speech; words obstruct the language of silence.'

'Words obstruct the language of silence,' Dana muttered under her breath.

This high philosophy was confusing; still Dana was fascinated by its imagery. The interplay between silence and speech was a contradiction, yet it seemed achievable. 'Such things can only happen in India,' Dana thought with a smile.

'What else should I look for besides silence?' she asked the swami.

'Love. What good is knowledge, what is the use of wisdom if there is no love? Good physique, knowledge and wisdom are nothing if there is no love. So look for love.'

'Anything else, Swami ji?' Dana asked eagerly, her pen hovering over her notebook. She had quickly transcribed all that because the swami charged by the minute.

'Nothing else, my child. It is very difficult to find a perfect guru these days. But if he has even 70 per cent of these qualities, you should grab that guru.'

The swami had also told her that the good gurus stayed in the mountains, away from the crowd.

■

This fix on the mountains of Rishikesh was an act of blind faith, because she did not have a rational explanation of how she had arrived at that conclusion. It was also an act of faith that had taken her on this long journey to a strange and complex country.

She should have rested in Rishikesh and spent a couple of days there, soaking in the sights and following the constant movement of the crowd. The bustle was such a contrast from her quiet life in Omaha. But she was fixated on finding her guru.

Despite the rush, she halted long enough to witness the morning puja by the Ganges before hungrily demolishing her first Indian meal of puri-chole followed by the extra sweet halwa.

Aping other customers, she, too, let out a satisfied burp to signal appreciation of the food she had eaten. Then, following their example, she moved her hand over her stomach in a gentle circular motion to settle the food she had just eaten. Like them, she also washed the ghee stains and bits of food off her hands by pouring a glass of water on her hands. She watched as water fell from her glass, through her hands, only to form an irregular stream on the road. Dana looked on with great interest as that stream lost its way in the dips and depressions of tar on that road.

All this was forbidden pleasure for her because you could get arrested in Omaha for washing your hands in a public place and littering the street. No wonder India was called the greatest democracy in action where people were free to do just as they fancied.

Though Dana was delighted by her Indian experience so far, she did have some trouble explaining to the other diners that her American town was actually called Omaha.

They did not believe her even when she pronounced each syllable carefully: O…M…A…H…A. They thought she was having fun with words and that she had made up the name of her town to rhyme with Osama, Obama or even Om!

'You mean Om?' some enquired in jest.

'No, Omaha.' She was careful not to mix the divine invocation and the name of a sleepy American town in the same breath.

'Om, Omaha—it is one and the same. You Americans like everything bigger! So you turned Om into Omaha,' one young boy insisted, relishing the sweet synchrony of the two sounds.

'No, no,' Dana protested, 'it is not Om, it is Omaha. It is

Warren Buffet's Omaha. Buffet is the swami of finance. People say he is an oracle of the stock markets. He and I are both from Omaha. He is rich, money gives him nirvana. But I am a simple girl looking for my soul.'

By the time she had finished her meal and completed the after-meal rituals like an Indian, shops were beginning to open in the bazaar. She hurried to a garment store and picked up two cotton sarees and two blouses to match. She also picked up a pair of leather sandals. This, she felt, was enough for her trip to the mountains.

The bus journey lasted for three hours. But it was far more exhausting than the 22 hours she had spent on the plane from the US and in the slow-moving train from Delhi. At last the bus dropped her in a small village, the last outpost before the steep climb by foot on a narrow mountain path.

Dana had no idea where she was going, nor any fixed destination; her sole objective was to seek the guru, whoever or wherever he was. On this note, she began to climb the mountain.

For the next two hours, she kept walking a few hundred yards up the winding path before stopping for a bit to catch her breath. But it was becoming more difficult to keep walking, the unpaved mountain road was getting steeper and narrower and the loose stones on it made it more difficult to walk on. As she went higher up the mountain, every breath became an effort. She felt her heart beat faster and louder. Many times she had the urge to lie down and sleep for a while. But she desisted; she was determined to cover as much distance as possible while it was still daytime.

Finally, she stopped near a rock.

A vast green valley full of thick vegetation and tall deodar trees stretched for miles below the rock. The entire region was at an elevation, and a cool breeze was blowing. After taking in some long and deep breaths of fresh air, Dana felt her tiredness go away.

'So far so good,' she muttered to herself. Then, she slowly scanned the rock. There, on the very top of it, she saw a nearly naked man sitting serenely. The ascetic seemed to be a striking presence, tranquil and in complete harmony with his surroundings.

'Hi,' Dana said conversationally, 'great life.'

'If I knew the meaning of life, would I be sitting on a cold rock in my loincloth?' The guru intoned from his lotus position on the bare rock.

Dana liked his honest answer. Her senses told her that this was it; that this loincloth-wearing ascetic was the guru she had travelled 10,000 miles for. He was the end of her quest; every pore in her body told her that she had reached her spiritual destination.

The man with the lustrous face sitting on top of the rock seemed godlike to her. The setting sun behind him was casting a golden halo around his head. He may not have been an exact replica of Krishna, yet she could see shades of divinity in him.

However, his cynical statement about the loincloth and the meaning of life puzzled her.

'I am wearing a saree and a blouse, still, I am shivering. You must have great willpower to sit there in your loincloth,' she tried again.

The guru on the rock smiled benignly.

'Mr Guru,' Dana continued, 'you must be a very content man.'

The guru closed his eyes and let out a long drawl, which sounded like a drawn-out 'Om' to Dana—the kind that only great yogis are capable of.

'What is your religion?' Dana asked, just to be sure that the man on the rock was a Hindu guru.

'Religion?' The semi-naked guru opened an enquiring eye. 'What is my religion? That is a difficult question to answer. It is like asking me to tell you who I am. People spend an entire lifetime and still they cannot say who they are. Even Buddha found that hard to answer. I am nothing in comparison.'

'Oh!' Dana said in awe.

'But if you are really keen to know my religion, then note that I belong to a truly evolved religion. My religion has been around for many thousand years. It is the religion of humanity. People like you and me have come together in all ages to make it richer. My religion is defined by what it permits, not by what it forbids. That is its greatness. Democracy of thought and freedom of action, this is my religion.'

'Love? What about love?' Dana blurted unwittingly. But a sudden rush of blood up her cheeks showed that she was embarrassed at having asked that question.

'Yes, love also. My religion loves love,' the guru said, looking directly into her eyes. 'Kamasutra is also my religion.'

'And Mr Guru, who is a friend for you?'

'Everyone'

'Everyone, Mr Guru?'

'Yes everyone. For me, a friend is someone you do not hate. Since I don't hate anyone in this world, everyone is my friend.'

'Oh, Mr Guru, I'm blessed,' Dana exclaimed ecstatically. 'Everything is so calm around here. In the midst of all this calmness, you are so profound. It is enough to make me cry.'

Then, overcome by emotion, she began to climb the rock to reach him. Her excitement at finally having found her guru was hastening her steps. But midway, she had to stop and get a better grip of her leather sandals, as she almost tripped over a crack in the rock surface.

When she reached the top of the rock, she hesitated. The swami in the US had warned her, 'Be careful. In America, people kiss in public and piss privately. But in India, it is the opposite. We piss in public but kiss privately.' So, shaking hands with the guru or bending forward to kiss him was out of question.

It was also quite normal in Omaha to slide on a sofa next to a man, but this was different. She could not share the rock with the great guru. So, Dana stepped back and selected a smaller rock to sit upon. This way, she could keep looking up to her guru.

She sat there for a long time, sharing his silence. Even in this quiet communication, she could feel great vibrations in their bodies. It was difficult to be relaxed in that position, but miraculously, the tension that she had experienced earlier disappeared. 'This must be the guru's doing,' Dana thought. It was then that she noticed his rippling muscles and a neat six-pack. He looked young too, despite his grey hair.

Dana's mental image of a holy man was of an ancient sage with unruly long grey hair and a free-flowing beard. But the guru sitting close to her had a stylishly trimmed beard and wavy hair. He looked handsome with his sharp features.

'You are great, Mr Guru.'

'You think so. But they don't,' he said, turning his face towards a temple on top of a nearby hill.

'Oh,' Dana responded non-committally.

This vague reaction troubled the guru. As an afterthought, he felt he had to be more forthcoming with her, because if he remained cryptic she would leave for the temple to seek answers from the people there.

'They are nothing,' the guru waved his hands dismissively towards that temple and added, 'they have absolutely no knowledge; very little gyan.'

'What is gyan, Mr Guru?'

'In my world, gyan means knowledge, even wisdom,' he clarified. 'A mixture of both actually. They have neither knowledge nor wisdom. But they have luck on their side; destiny favours them. The temple gives them status. People flock there thinking that since they are living in a big temple they must be important holy men, full of wisdom.'

'Are they?' Dana enquired.

'Bums! That is what they are, doped out bums. Total frauds, if you ask me.' The guru exploded, 'They know nothing of the holy books. I am literate, a graduate. I completed my college, only then I took to the mountains. When I read the Gita, I understand it. They can't even write their names in English.'

'Why do they bother you so, Mr Guru? You are a holy man, you have your own beat. You should be content with that.'

'How can I be content when they sit above me?' The guru snorted, 'I am also human. I want to be the biggest guru around here, after all, I have my ego, my ambition.'

Ego! Ambition! All this was the stuff of lesser mortals— people who were not evolved, who lacked the right material. Throughout her journey from New York to Delhi, and then during the train journey from Delhi to Rishikesh, she had been reading Hindu scriptures. Each one of them had a common central message—the ultimate aim of all living beings should be moksh; the complete renunciation of all that is worldly.

A guru was truly a guru when he reached that stage, or was almost there. Yet, here was this guru talking of his ego and ambition. This caused great dialectical confusion for her. 'How could want and renunciation coexist?' Dana wondered, shaking her head. Without moving from her position, Dana spoke in a gentle tone, 'Ego! Ambition! But why, Mr Guru? Why should you think of such things? You should be above it all.'

'Ha!' the guru laughed, 'Easier said than done. Try living under these jokers on the hill and then you will understand.'

He gave Dana a long lingering look and added, 'There are so many temptations in life. Even gods are not above jealousies— neither your Christian Gods nor our Hindu Gods. Ego and ambition must be mastered, but they are also the spices of life. They determine human destiny.'

'Ego and ambition determine destiny or destiny shapes them? Tell me, Mr Guru, I am confused.'

'It's not your fault—everyone in this kalyug is confused. That's our destiny, our pre-written karma,' the guru intoned. 'You see, the celestial hierarchy is the cause of all confusion. It leads to jealousies and fights, but it also makes this world and the afterlife interesting. Otherwise, uniformity would be so boring.'

'As for me,' he added, looking directly into her eyes, 'I am in the transition stage. I am far from being evolved. I am still prey to temptation.'

'Oh Mr Guru, that is so profound. You are just like Krishna. Like him, you are prey to temptation. That's great.'

The guru smiled. 'Don't forget that I am also human. How can I sit here contentedly and watch a non-stop procession of men and women going there day in and day out, just to be duped by those thugs? Meanwhile, I sit here all day, all alone, just by myself, and meditate on the meaning of life. No one comes to me because I do not have a fixed address. You see, even gurus need a calling card, a location the devotees can relate to. Having a temple gives status and respectability to a guru.'

'Why don't you buy a temple, Mr Guru?'

Dana wanted to add that she could sell her apartment in Omaha and raise money for a temple. But then, she remembered that there was a recession in the housing sector in the US and it was difficult to get a decent price for property.

On the contrary, and going by what the guru had just said about the clamour for temples, it might be easier to sell a temple in the Himalayas and buy an apartment from that money in Omaha. But she banished the mischievous thought from her mind with a quick shake of her head. 'I must not think of money in Mr Guru's presence,' she reminded herself severely.

The guru was silent for a long time. His eyes had an otherworldly look as he began to focus on some distant object. Steadily, his face began to reflect a new glow as if Lord Krishna himself had entered his body.

Dana was enthralled; she kept looking at him, spellbound. If a moment can be called a turning point, where a person is said to have absolutely and irretrievably fallen in love, this was that moment for Dana.

She was ready to do anything for her playful Divine.

At last, the guru came back among the living. The faraway look was gone and he turned to look at her, 'You asked why I don't have a temple of my own. You could call it bad karma. Or maybe I have the wrong horoscope. You tell me, what is your guess?' The guru asked softly, leaning towards the rock she was sitting on. He could now inhale the soft lavender perfume she was wearing.

'Frankly, I am bewildered. You are so human at one level especially when you admit to your temptations. Yet, at another level, you are divine,' Dana said softly.

The guru smiled contentedly, and signalled her to get up and sit by him to share his rock.

Dana's face lit up. She slid forward and prostrated herself at the guru's feet. He could now see deep into the blouse that was several sizes too big for her.

'Rise, Dana,' the guru whispered huskily.

'Rise,' he repeated, moving close to her and gently pushing her up. Dana could feel his warm breath on her neck as his arms began to circle her waist, pulling her closer. They remained entwined on the rock for a long time.

Later, he told her that she had taken the first step towards her moksh.

When she asked him what that meant, he replied, 'Freedom. Now, like me, you can sit in your underpants on a rock and search for the meaning of life.'

$\mathcal{S}$illy girl,' Shyam declared gravely.

'She was gullible,' I added.

'Gullible, silly, rebellious or whatever, I do not know,' Shiv replied defensively.

He had the habit of averting his gaze when he was cagey, which according to me was the case most of the time.

'I suppose it would be unfair to single her out,' Shyam said.

'Most young people are restless; otherwise millions of hippies would not have flooded India in the '70s. Some stayed on, others became wiser by that experience and went back to do great things in life. Steve Jobs was one such person. But there were many others who ended up very confused; they could neither belong here nor go back to their roots,' Shiv explained. 'Dana was adventurous at that point in her life. Before she had left for India, I had told her bluntly that these gurus were our cocktail shakers, mixing up a bit of hope and a dash of cheer. But she had been in no mood to listen.'

I guess he was right because youths like Dana usually end

up being rootless and ruthlessly unattached. They are gypsies without air miles. I had had many deep discussions with flower children like Dana without arriving anywhere. After many such marathons, I had understood that arrival was the least among their priorities; it was the journey that fascinated them. They wanted to float free, so how could a person like Dana settle down?

'She left you for that guru? Weren't you good enough?' Shyam persisted. 'You must have been bitter?'

'Why should I be bitter? It is her life, she can do what she wants with it,' Shiv answered calmly. 'Incidentally, no one left anyone. We simply outgrew each other.'

'Are you in touch?' Shyam asked, rephrasing his question, a little gently this time.

'I shifted to Chicago. Had I been living somewhere close to Omaha, I would have continued to dissuade her and told her frankly that these gurus are no good. On the other hand, it is good that she discovered things for herself. She suffered a few knocks in the process, and that guru must have had great sex for a few months. But at the end of it, her dream of floating free was over. She is back again at her old job in Omaha, and we keep in touch off and on.'

He thought for a while before adding, 'She is still a restless soul. One day she wants to open a café, the next day she is all excited by a new idea of joining a jazz group. The day after, she forgets about everything else and gets busy planning a street party. Her nervous energy fascinates me, but her lack of focus disappoints me. There is no stability in her life; she flits constantly. Even if I had tried one more time, our relationship wouldn't have lasted.'

'Not many do,' I interjected in a rare tart comment against Shiv.

Just then, I was reminded of Mrs Keeling. She could turn an ordinary conversation into a philosophical event by making the most profound statement.

Once, she had remarked casually, 'Who can erase what destiny has written on your brow?' I had pondered over that for many days, tossing the statement this way and that in my mind. Now, after so many years, I had the practical proof in Shiv and his philandering ways. He loved the company of women. Our Shiv was an incorrigible romantic. He could never find fault in a young and good-looking woman.

'It is written on your brow,' I said softly, echoing Mrs Keeling.

■

'Did you…' Shyam started, but left the rest unsaid.

Shyam had probably wanted to ask something personal, but just as the unasked was on the tip of his tongue, he had reconsidered. He was too gentle to ask anything hurtful.

Shiv was watching him carefully, a smile beginning to dance on his lips. 'Did you…' he repeated like his brother, before quickly changing course. 'Do you miss things you leave behind?' he asked me.

'Well,' I began, stalling, 'the past is a trauma.'

'You mean remembering the past is a trauma,' Shyam added helpfully.

I nodded in agreement, giving Shiv the opening he needed. 'If you don't like remembering the past, it means you can think of other things.'

'Other things?'

'I mean other women. You couldn't have spent all your adult life thinking of Sati?' Shiv prodded.

He knew this was exactly how it was. Sati and her memory had haunted me all my adult life. I had kept pocketing withered dreams every single day of my life.

'There were other women,' Shiv insisted.

'There was nothing of the sort, just passing encounters.'

'Really?' Shiv chirped, excitement colouring his cheeks red.

'Like this girl from Botswana.'

'Oh,' Shyam joined in, curiously.

'There was nothing there. But, oh, it was interesting meeting her,' I said, beginning my story.

seventeen

Sat

$\mathcal{S}$ he was the last to board the flight, almost delaying the plane. It must have meant rushing through the airport checks and running down the departure hall to catch the flight, but she showed no sign of that stress. She looked cheerful as she traipsed down the aisle, throwing sunny smiles both ways. Right and left, right and left—it went on like this to mechanical perfection. If you also took in her dress—a short black skirt and a crisply starched white shirt—it was easy to mistake her for an off-duty airhostess who was habitually spreading cheer among passengers.

I was sitting close to the tail, almost at the rear of the aircraft. Still, she came all the way to my row and leaned across the empty aisle seat to ask, 'Hi. Do you mind shifting? I always take the window seat.'

The aircraft was not full; there were many empty rows she

could have picked a window seat from. Why did she walk all the way, down to where I was sitting, to ask me to vacate my seat? I was a window-seat freak myself, I liked looking at the passing clouds and the changing landscape below.

I should have refused to shift. I should have told her I was sitting in my rightful place. But she began fluttering her eyes, so I got up and shuffled to the aisle seat.

'You are sweet,' she said, tapping me on my arm with her fingernails.

That was it. She thanked me coquettishly, and having done me that one favour, she turned abruptly to look out of the window. Frankly speaking, it left me feeling like a discarded tissue paper.

'Why do you think I chose this seat?' she asked after a while.

'I was wondering about that.'

'This seat overlooks the luggage hold and I wanted to see that my luggage had actually been loaded.'

Her obsession with the luggage seemed weird to me.

'Johannesburg airport has a terrible reputation, you know,' she continued. 'The chances are that your luggage may not be on your flight.'

'Why would they do that?'

'It happens nine out of ten times. You can ask others,' she concluded, flashing that sensuous smile again.

I had no intention of asking anyone, but her doubt had made me anxious. What if my luggage was not on board?

'You know why it happens?' she asked.

'Tell me.'

'Because they hate us.'

'All South Africans hate your people?' I asked, surprised.

'Not all of them. Not all the time. But you could say that a majority don't like us,' she said, toning it down. 'Now, you might ask me their motivation. Why do they hate us? These are legitimate questions, and so are my answers to them. My reply is simple. It is because they envy our diamonds.'

'Oh,' I responded. I knew Botswana produced some fine diamonds. But so did South Africa, and in far greater quantities. So why would it envy its smaller neighbour's dose of good fortune?

'It is funny actually,' she shrugged. 'This goes back to the colonial times when South Africa and Botswana were one. Ours was the poorer part. Hardly anything grew here because of the Kalahari Desert. We lived on doles from South Africa. Still, at a certain point, our chiefs demanded that Botswana be carved out as a separate state. The white rulers thought it was a damn good idea; they would get rid of a financial drain. So, they agreed—noblesse obliged.'

What she told me corresponded to what I had read about the area. A rare visitor to Botswana had described it as a dump, a desolate and grim place. There was hardly any industrial activity, very little agriculture, and nothing when it came to mineral wealth. When it became independent, it was known largely for its lack of sanitation facilities, its excellent beef and for the black mamba snake. The last item on the list was the deadliest snake in the world.

'But men in Botswana are deadlier,' she said. 'As soon as he gets up in the morning, every Botswana man thanks his god. It was by god's design that the huge diamond reserves in Botswana were discovered only after we became independent. Had the South African whites known of that potential we would never have gotten our independence.'

'Your men thank god. They must do something else?'

She smiled, showing two rows of perfectly formed milky white teeth. I noticed then that her body glistened in the sunlight filtering through the window. Hers was an alluring mix of ebony and ivory. She was several shades lighter than ebony but many tones darker than ivory—an exciting colour tone.

'I didn't get your name,' I asked.

'Margaret. And by the way, how would you know my name if I did not tell you?' she replied, flashing those teeth again. 'Incidentally, you must remain nameless till the end of the journey. Then, if we like each other, I will ask you for your name.'

She had some strange rules, but I played along to pass my time. Margaret told me the story of her life in the next thirty minutes; that she had fallen in love, had gotten carried away and had a baby.

'And then?'

'Then what? I was left holding the baby,' she laughed, as if it was a great joke.

Being positive was a great quality. But this was taking optimism a bit too far. It was none of my business so I kept my counsel to myself.

'All of it happened quickly. Before I could realize the enormity of it, I was left stranded on the rough road of life, with nowhere to go. Sometimes I feel like I have been standing at the fork of that road all my life.' Margaret added whimsically, 'You might ask what I did there.'

Instead, I asked, 'You never got married?'

'Should one? Must one?' Margaret responded, a slight smile playing on her lips.

'Almost all do,' I made the statistical assertion.

'Not everyone. All don't get married,' she said with a dismissive wave of her hand.

'You should have married,' I insisted. 'He had a responsibility after making you pregnant.'

'Men in Botswana are fair, they don't shirk their responsibility. He pays the maintenance money regularly for the child.'

She was either a very talented actress or a hugely optimistic person. If she felt betrayed, or had any regret, it did not show in her manner. How could she call a man's callous behaviour fair?

'The man got away lightly. He pays a pittance and then he is free to play the field again,' I asserted.

'That's life,' she shrugged. 'If I was given the choice I would never marry,' Margaret declared.

'If marriage was compulsory, who would you marry?'

'If marriage was compulsory,' she repeated, mimicking my Indian accent, 'then my dear new friend, I would marry an old man. The older, the better.'

'You would marry an old man? But why?' I asked in a voice shriller than I had intended.

'Old men die quickly,' she said, looking straight into my eyes, 'They are gentle, and they treat women with dignity. It is possible to have a relationship with an old man, a good short-term relationship that doesn't let you get bored.'

'I see,' I responded, scratching my head.

'Have you heard of crimes of passion?' she asked suddenly.

'No,' I shook my head.

'Don't you have that in India?' she asked, unable to understand what I meant. 'Crimes of passion take place when a man clobbers a woman to death.'

'There are some cases. But it is rare,' I said defensively.

'Our Botswana male is easily agitated. He suspects readily. Just a glance, a friendly handshake with another man is enough to set his alarm bells ringing.'

'Don't you have a MeToo movement in Botswana?' I asked.

'Are you holding a quiz?' Margaret smirked.

'No, no. Please continue.'

'Suspicion begins to gnaw at him. He keeps knocking it about in his head, imagining the worst, a fling at the very least. Once he starts agitating in this manner, he reaches for the beer. One after the other, he keeps opening and drinking cans of beer. Meanwhile, he does not let his agitated mind rest, the overdrive continues.'

'Oh.'

'That's nothing. Wait till you hear the rest,' Margaret said impatiently.

I could notice a slight tremble in her hands as if some great agitation had taken hold of her. Her voice was shriller than before and blood had rushed to her cheeks, adding a third colour to the ebony and ivory mix of her skin.

'That harmless look, the extra warm handshake or worse still, a fling, becomes a full-fledged affair in that beer-induced haze of the man,' Margaret continued. 'His eyes widen and his grip on the beer becomes tighter, and tighter still. This is a warning signal.'

Margaret's voice dropped to a whisper now. For the first time, there were drops of perspiration on her face, an ugly reminder perhaps of a personal nightmare.

'Then?'

'The woman tries to stay as far as possible from him, in the kitchen, in the toilet or better still, out in the garden.'

'But these are temporary sanctuaries,' I said, anticipating the worst.

'Sooner or later, she has to cross his path. She knows it, and this fear makes her sweat. The sweating starts first in her armpits and then large drops begin to form on her face. She keeps wiping them, but some manage to trickle down from her forehead to the corners of her eyes, preceding the tears.'

Margaret sounded like she was describing a hunted animal—a deer who was tired of running away and knew the inevitability of being torn apart by the chasing lion.

'At about this point, the crime of passion begins. The beer-sozzled man gets up unsteadily from his chair and lunges forward towards wherever she is hiding. Sweat begins to pour down his face too. But he is not sweating out of fear, he sweats in venom. His armpits are soaked with sweat—that pungent smell is the smell of the gutter.'

'She should run,' I whispered, gripping the armrest. 'Why can't she run?'

'Around this time he spots her in her hiding place. He looks around quickly to see if there are any escape routes, and rushes to that door to block her exit. Having successfully trapped her, he bares his teeth. This isn't a Dracula-like thirst for blood, it is cannibalistic quest.'

'Oh my god,' I sighed, anticipating the worst.

Margaret's face mirrored the horror as if she was the hunted woman, or as if she was reliving what she had gone through once. Blood seemed to have drained out of her face, turning it ash white. Her voice had a sense of urgency; it was now a plea for help.

'The woman slinks to the furthest corner, her lips dry up and her eyes bulge in horror,' Margaret continued. 'There is a faint prayer on her lips, the last desperate plea to god to somehow save her.'

'Doesn't the man stop?'

'The man roars threats and obscenities at her, challenging her to defy him. But challenge is not an option for her. Tears well up in her eyes, she folds her hands and pleads. This provokes him further. At this point, the woman manages to say, "I didn't do no wrong." That desperate plea becomes the trigger. He lunges forward, both his arms spread ahead of him. Then he opens his hands and points them towards her like a pair of poisoned claws.'

I've never had the stomach for horror stories. On the odd occasion when someone related one to me, I spend the entire night having nightmares.

'Can't we talk about something else?' I requested.

'You have to listen to this,' Margaret insisted. 'The woman

knows instinctively which part of the body he will aim for.'

'Why? How would she know? She has no previous experience,' I asked.

'It's a part of the local lore. Most crimes of passion happen the same way; men behave predictably and so do women. The woman puts both her hands around her neck and lets out a shriek. The neighbours hear her, but no one ever interferes in a crime of passion. Soon the man's hands find their target. It is said that alcohol saps strength, but in this case the man feels a sudden burst of energy in his body, alcohol becomes the fuel for gore and he grabs her neck in a steadily tightening grip.'

'Please stop it,' I urged, 'I don't want to hear anymore.'

But Margaret carried on as if she needed to get the poison out of her system.

'People say eyes are the mirror of the soul, that eyes do not lie,' she said. 'It must be true, because at that point the woman's eyes reflect a mixture of fear and disbelief. She still can't believe that it is happening to her. How can he forget the good times they have shared? Was his show of love a mere deception? All these and other thoughts pass through her mind in a lightning flash. Then, as the grip becomes vice-like, she screams a final time. Just one last fading screech of a scratched gramaphone record.'

'Stop it please,' I pleaded again.

But she ignored me. Completing her story of murder had acquired a life of its own—a catharsis.

'Her soul escapes the body then. Her world ends; what were once her strong enchantments now lie frozen in time, a dead weight in his hands. The irreversibility of his act finally hits the weight in his hands. The irreversibility of his act finally hits the killer. He slackens his grip slowly, his faithless hands loosen their hold to let the body slide to the ground,' Margaret sighed. She looked spent, as if she had gone through an exhausting ordeal.

'What does the man do then? Does he run away?'

'It varies. Some run away, others wait for the police to arrive. Invariably, even those who run away from the scene of murder get caught. Almost everyone ends up spending a lifetime in prison. But the man does not care. The main thing for him is that he has preserved his dignity, whatever that means.'

'Do women ever commit crimes of passion?' I asked.

'Not really,' she replied slowly, as if she was doing a mental check to confirm that what she was saying was statistically correct, 'There may be an odd case here or there. But that's about it because it is physically not possible. How can a woman kill a man? We are not strong enough nor are we driven to anger quickly. Unfortunately, women are weak and passive.'

'So how do women react to infidelity?'

'When we discover infidelity, we sulk. All that remains of the relationship thereafter is resentment.'

'It takes two to clap, doesn't it?'

She mulled over that, trying to think it through. Her feminist side militating against the implication that willing women are necessary for infidelity. At last, the cobwebs seemed to have cleared.

'There can be multiple partners and there can be abstinence. I find nothing wrong with either. The point I am making is that men are basically insecure. They are constantly worried that a lover may be lurking behind their woman's skirt.'

'Don't be silly.'

'That's a fact,' she insisted loudly, startling other passengers. 'Do you know why the brave soldiers of our army refuse to go out on military exercises that last more than three months?'

I shook my head lamely.

'One month or even two months are okay. But anything beyond that means crossing the line of temptation. Such a long absence could tempt a woman to stray. They feel it is bad enough to leave her behind when the world is full of preying Lotharios. But a long absence is an invitation to disaster, it is sure to sway her.' She took a pause before adding, 'Now tell me, if these tough-looking army guys are so insecure, what must happen to ordinary men?'

Then, she craned her head over the seat to look around. But she couldn't readily spot a man who fitted the description she had in mind. Finally, she turned around and looked at me critically to say, 'Ordinary men like you.'

I was devastated. I had never considered myself ordinary in any department. Yet, here was my acquaintance of just about one hour who had already assessed and pronounced that I was ordinary, just another Tom, Dick or Harry. I shrank insignificantly into my seat, and at that moment, I must have looked ordinary. It was probably because of the desire to avenge this insult that I asked her bluntly, 'So what is your choice in life? Will you marry?'

'I'm not sure. Probably I will. But if I marry, I'll marry an old man.'

Since I was smarting from her remark about being ordinary, I asked, 'If you can't marry an old man?'

'Then I will remain a free bird.'

We were within the sight of Gaberone. Our aircraft had begun to circle low over a vast brown landscape, and it had also given Margaret the time to decide.

'To tell you the truth,' she said gravely, 'I would rather be bitten by a black mamba than marry a mamba male.'

I just had the time to say 'Oh!' because by then we had landed. As we got up to leave the aircraft, we shook hands warmly. I thought she might ask my name then, but she smiled and carried on.

$\mathscr{I}$t was close to seven, still an hour away from the time I usually began drinking in Delhi. But this was different. We were meeting in Mussoorie after so many years, and unlike in Delhi, evening shadows began spreading early in Mussoorie.

Had Mrs Keeling been with us, she would have insisted, 'Don't gossip so much, boys. You need to lubricate your throats. Otherwise, with the amount of yapping you are doing, you might damage a throat muscle. Come, get yourself a drink before you go on.'

Thinking of her, I said, 'We have been talking continuously for the past three hours. I need a drink.'

'You just had tea,' Shiv ribbed.

'This is drinking time. In Mrs Keeling's house, that's the priority,' I insisted.

For once, Shiv did not yell '*koi hai*' to call out a servant. This time, he went in himself to pull out the drinks trolley.

'I should report you to Alcoholics Anonymous,' Shiv mocked. 'But don't give it a thought while we are here. Drink the entire barrel before I produce you at the AA meeting in Delhi.'

Shiv was right about waiting for us to reach Delhi to get me to AA, because AA would not have gotten office space in Mussoorie. Everyone here was a dedicated drinker. And so was I. As with Mrs Keeling, that was priority for me too. Like her I was also a discerning drinker. Just any ordinary hooch would not do for me. I did make an exception occasionally, but if malt was available in the house then I would settle for nothing else and nothing less. At Mrs Keeling's, a bottle of malt whisky was always available.

In our schooldays, we were not allowed anything stronger than an occasional beer, but we sometimes managed to steal a peg or two from Mrs Keeling's malt whiskies. Having had so much malt in Mrs Keeling's house, I looked accusingly at Shiv.

'Now what? Do you expect me to pour your bloody drink?'

'No, thank you, that will not be necessary,' I smiled.

'Then what? Did I miss out on the pink champagne?' Shiv scowled.

'Malt, my friend. You forgot the malt.'

'Oh, bloody hell. How stupid of me?' Shiv slapped his forehead with his right palm and rushed in again. He emerged triumphantly a moment later and handed over the bottle to me. 'Now, can we get on with the next story?'

I took my time pouring out a stiff drink. Then, I set about with the precision of a surgeon in selecting the right ice cube. After discarding a number of odd-shaped cubes, I selected one small cube, which would just about lower the temperature of the whisky by one degree. That suited my taste perfectly.

'Should I pour out drinks for you?' I asked Shyam and Shiv.

'We will do it ourselves.'

They poured themselves extra-large portions, not of malt, but of the regular Indian whisky. They said they missed its kick abroad. Shyam rolled the first sip in his mouth, relishing its pungency. Then, he surprised us by saying, 'The art of losing is hard to master.'

Both Shiv and I looked up from the rims of our glasses. Before we could ask him why, he added even more mysteriously, 'In the harshest moments of my suffering, I have always held the hope that someone up there would rescue me.'

Shiv was the first to ask anxiously, 'Why do you say that?'

'You have both told stories of how women suffer. But men can also have complaints.'

'Tell us about them,' Shiv prompted.

Shyam was generally a closed book. Unlike Shiv, he did not talk much. But this time, he surprised us by unwinding quickly.

nineteen

Shyam

Shyam began from the very beginning. There were questions that came to my mind as I heard him, but I decided not to ask them because they would have interrupted the flow. I have not distorted in the least bit what he told us, in the version I am relating below.

The name 'Shyam', he said, reflected his parents' wish of seeing him grow with a saintly air about him. Throughout this youth, they used to make him stand every morning in front of the framed pictures of two divines in the living room. One was that of a mystically smiling Krishna, the other was a picture of Christ nailed to the cross.

When he would position himself precisely in the middle, right under them, he would be required to light two incense sticks—one for each god. Then, as the incense-filled smoke would spiral up, his parents would point with reverential pride towards the framed gods and say, 'See, this is where faith can take you.'

Shyam did not fancy the idea of being framed, and hung on a wall, but he would never argue with his parents. Instead, he would nod obediently.

One time, they were vacationing in Nainital—a hill station like Mussoorie, but built around a lake. Shyam loved the outdoors and hiked as much as he could. A hill station was ideal for a hiker with its mountains and valleys, streams and orchards. And though Shiv was scared of the idea of ghosts, Shyam was curious about the mountains.

Tales about the supernatural interested him because of their sense of intrigue and mystery. Since he was curious by nature, he liked to investigate and question.

His parents did not mind those walks and hikes, nor did they discourage him from pursuing the supernatural, but they forbade him from visiting a neighbouring orchard because of a local legend. It was said that a ghost inhabited a tamarind tree in the middle of the orchard, and anyone who went near the tree annoyed the ghost, and he or she ended up dead within a week.

When Shyam asked his parents what was so special about a tamarind tree that ghosts rested there, they said, 'Shut up, the ghost can hear you.'

He wanted to point out that if all the tamarind trees of the world were occupied by ghosts and for that reason were out of reach for the living, no one would ever get any tamarind to eat. But he decided against asking the question.

The fact of the matter was that Mr and Mrs Keeling were very conservative in some respects, and in such matters, they imposed a restrictive regime. Shyam felt cramped by their diktat during those formative years; he found it hard to reconcile his inquisitive mind with their obstinate faith.

For a brief moment, during that vacation in Nainital, he thought of standing his ground and pointing out the flaw in their argument about the tamarind tree. But it was a hopeless task. They were rigid in their belief and the most innocuous enquiry was enough to raise their hackles. The simplest 'why' about religion irritated them; they viewed it suspiciously, judging it to be a challenging probe, one that could be followed by more fundamental doubts. After putting up some initial resistance, he fell in line and did not go anywhere near the orchard with the tamarind tree. Once more their faith had won.

This is how it always was. As a result, he was a prude even during his college days, perpetually conscious of his parents' faith, and in great awe of their gods. Consequently, he would close his eyes, fold his hands, and bow his head respectfully the moment someone mentioned a god's name, or if a statue or an image of some god happened to cross his line of vision.

On the rare occasion when god was not looking over his shoulders, there was the fear of upsetting his parents. Sometimes he had the feeling that god was his parents' creation to trap him.

The Keelings were liberal by temperament and they always encouraged debate. Yet, it did not prevent them from trying to temper him into polished steel. Shyam was the older sibling, and the Keelings must have exhausted all their energy on him.

As a result Shiv had a relatively freer hand on how he managed his affairs.

After college, Shyam went to Bombay to take up his first job. It was his great escape, because at last, he was on his own. There was no one around to ensure that he bowed his head every morning to photo-framed gods hung on the wall.

Soon god and he began to inhabit different planets. He was happily settled in Bombay and god was living somewhere up above. Now, Shyam nodded at him only occasionally, and that too, when he had a bad day at office. But Shyam did miss his parents.

Sometimes, when he was tipsy and alone at night, he would sob softly into his pillow and think of them. By the time he would wake up the next morning, he would forget all about his tears—he would be a changed man again.

Bombay was also the place where he learned many lessons of life. Among these, he found betrayal the toughest to forget.

∎

The big change in Bombay took place on his first day at work. Shyam stepped into a new world when he reported for work at the advertising agency.

'Name?' the boss enquired busily when he walked gingerly into his office room.

'Shyam, Sir,' Shyam said, nervously.

'Sham!' the boss repeated mechanically without looking at Shyam. 'That's new! Well, Sham, your name is your business. But we guys don't sham around here, we slog. Is that clear?'

Before Shyam could reply, he asked, 'Do you know this lady here?'

'No, Sir.'

'Sham,' the boss snapped, pointing towards Shyam. Then he looked at a woman in the room and whispered, 'Shwe, she is Shwe.'

He stopped, merely to scratch the back of his head, and added, 'Shwe joined two minutes before you did. She was right on time. So, she will be your senior in the company. Do not ever forget that if you want to get ahead in life, you will have to be on time. Not just on time, rather ahead of time to be ahead of others. Ahead of time, to be ahead of others. How marvellous,' he repeated, chuckling at his turn of phrase.

'Yes, Sir,' Shyam nodded. But he was beginning to wonder if he had already lost the race of life.

The boss waved him out of the room with a flick of his hand. That was it, just a dismissive turn of the hand. After that, Shyam ceased to exist for him. But, as he was turning to leave, Shyam noticed that the boss was pouring tea for the lady who had joined the office two minutes before him.

The boss also said that Shwe and he were going to share an office room. Shyam went there directly, she walked in a good thirty minutes later; her mysterious smile made him wonder what had transpired between her and the boss.

'Hi, I'm Shwe,' she chirped, gliding into the room.

Back home in Mussoorie, white people did not shake hands with non-white girls for fear of offending them and their parents, their fathers in particular. So, Shyam looked at her extended hand hesitantly. But then, he realized he could not remain rooted to the past forever. This was Bombay and here he had to move with time. Thus, encouraged, he got up and grabbed her hand.

Shyam's handshake was firm and bone-crunching. Shwe was fragile, she screamed as he pressed her hand hard. Shyam must have said sorry a thousand times before moving guiltily into his chair.

'Suicide?' Shwe asked.

'No,' Shyam replied, his face flushed with young passion.

He knew in that instant that they would either end up as lovers or he would have to move to another room in the office.

He would long remember the butter-like softness of her hand. Till then, he had not known what a female hand felt like, except that of his mother. His mother's hands were weather-beaten from years of pottering around in the garden. Shwe's were delicate, fragile enough to be folded like a handkerchief.

There was another thing that made a great impression on him that first day in office. After he got over the embarrassment of hurting her hand, he became conscious of the perfumed air around her. A sweet-sour combination of tuberose and lemon had spread in the room. This sophisticated smell was a new experience for him because in his small-town college, the predominantly male population used to identify each other by distinctive body odours. Sharp, pungent smells trailed them everywhere. In contrast, Shwe and her perfume was otherworldly.

That night, he repeated the two names, like a mantra. 'Sham-Shwe,' he kept saying hopefully. He was also quick to get used to his new name. Shyam, Sham—it meant the same to him now.

However, this change to a big city was not all smooth. The most difficult part was to spend the evenings and the long nights that followed alone.

In those lonely spells, he realized that he was being sucked into a perilous passion. Many ghosts haunted him, and so feverish were his imaginations that he often woke up exhausted.

Sometimes, he thought of acts of great chivalry, deeds that would make Shwe forget the boss and fall in love with him. His favourite scene was this:

He is walking down an office corridor when Shwe has a fainting spell. He is walking half a step behind her when she staggers, about to fall down on the hard ground. But he reacts quickly, and instead of the hard ground, she lands in the soft cradle of his arms. She rests there gratefully and from his arms, she gives him a look of pure love.

This movie-like encounter was all fantasy, of course, but it never failed to boost him. Thus, energized, he would walk into the office, floating on cloud nine, only to find that his cheery 'good morning' would echo in an empty room. Like always, Shwe would be in the boss's cabin for the morning coffee.

Still, Shyam continued to live in hope.

One day, he got lucky and found himself sitting with Shwe in the office canteen. She ordered a glass of milk and coke. Shyam had drank a lifetime's supply of milk in Mussoorie, but he still ordered the same combination. When their drinks arrived, she poured her coke into the glass of cold milk. He did the same.

Then, she took a deep sip and blew it back with some force into the straw, creating a virtual storm of bubbles in her glass.

Shyam, too, blew into his glass, and to his surprise, he found that he liked the thrill and the taste of it. They were like children, alternately sipping and blowing through the straw and having a good time together. At some point, they looked at each other and burst out laughing. This was the most precious moment of his young life. He felt that something special might have begun to brew between them.

■

Over the next few days, he felt an intimacy developing between them; even their silences seemed to be as meaningful as their stolen glances. Shyam felt she was reciprocating his feelings. There was just one fly in the ointment. The boss continued to call her frequently to his office.

Since he was new to city life, he did not know how to react. But his intuition was that the boss was up to no good. There were many occasions when he would jump out of his chair with the idea of thrashing the daylights out of his boss. At the last moment, however, he would think of his job and slink back into the chair. But he continued to pursue Shwe. Once, when they were leaving office, he suggested that they stop by at a café.

'Why not?' she responded cheerfully.

When they walked to their table, at the far end of the restaurant, all eyes—male as well as female—followed her. She was wearing a rust coloured saree that did wonders to her complexion. Her luxuriant hair danced on her shoulders as she walked daintily on high heels. Shwe was a tall girl and had the grace of a model, so it was natural for her to receive attention.

Shyam felt proud that he was walking by her side. When they found a free table in the busy café, he said, 'Thank god.'

'Thank god indeed that he is not here,' Shwe responded.

'Hunn…huu,' he chanted non-committally.

'Just imagine the complication it would cause if he was here with us,' Shwe added teasingly.

'Hunn,' he grunted, a little uncertainly this time.

'One thing even you should acknowledge readily is the fact that he is the greatest manager the world has ever had.'

Shwe was not one for half measures. Her sentences would be extra-long, as if she wanted to complete whatever she had to say in one go. As a result, she would often sound breathless. The other thing was her habit of going for absolutes—what she said had to be the last word on the subject.

'Just think what would happen if he was here with us,' she was playing a subtle game, but Shyam was unable to understand it.

'You mean between us?'

'No, not here, just among us,' Shwe waved her hand to include the entire room.

'Why the hell can't he leave us alone?' Shyam fumed.

'Millions, billions, are in awe of him. They worship him,' Shwe carried on.

'Worship?' Shyam repeated, bewildered. Was she serious about billions worshipping an advertising manager? Wasn't she going over the top?

'Imagine if he was here.'

'People would stop drinking their coffee. They would probably kneel down on their knees to worship him,' he said testily.

'Just imagine,' Shwe chirped, before adding more soberly, 'but some people can be vicious. They would file a FIR against him for disorderly conduct.'

'He could be jailed,' Shyam said, relishing the prospect.

'Can you imagine the scene? Actually seeing him here with us, between us.'

Shyam didn't share her enthusiasm.

'Just think if god was here, between us,' she pointed to the small space that Shyam had reluctantly left between them.

'Let's order,' he suggested finally.

Later that night, when he was in his paying guest accommodation, two corresponding thoughts came to his mind. First, if she was thinking of the real god, then the boss was not that high up the love ladder. Second, it meant that Shyam still had a chance. Relieved, he turned off the light. Lying happily in bed, he let his imagination soar up to the point of a grand wedding.

They had their first disagreement the next morning.

It was a minor matter that triggered the argument. Shyam was telling her about Mussoorie and the simple people back there. She kept listening patiently, but in the end, she said, 'The class difference shows.'

She had not finished yet, because she looked at him critically and added, 'A person's background makes all the difference. Look at our boss, he is so sophisticated.'

When they were leaving their office that evening, Shyam did not suggest that they stop by for coffee. As a matter of fact, they never went out together again. Shyam was still like a calf, deeply infatuated with her, but the intense ardour was missing.

Shyam continued to be in love; she made him go weak in the knees every time she looked at him. But he was also beginning to see through her lies and evasions. Her extended trips to the boss's office riled him the most.

What the boss did, who he favoured, was his business. But the off-hand, dismissive manner in which he had begun to deal with Shyam rankled him. Moreover, he did not like the way Shwe reacted every time she was called to the boss's office.

Her face would light up, she would reach for her purse, apply an unnecessary extra line of lip liner, and wriggle her hips most obscenely to get out of her chair as she danced out of their shared room towards his office.

It was not as if Shyam was lacking in any way, he was probably better-looking and more skilled. But he couldn't change the fact that the other person was born a few years ahead of him, and because of that circumstance, he was the boss. His position in the office was her aphrodisiac. But she also kept Shyam hanging on a hopeful string, encouraging him to believe in miracles.

A year later, they were both confirmed in service by the company. Around that time, the company also announced its annual transfers to different parts of India. Shyam was the only one in the office who was surprised when the boss and Shwe were transferred to the same city, away from Bombay.

A month later, he received a formal invitation to their wedding.

■

Shyam did not wallow in misery, but he felt like Shwe had taken him for a ride. This led to his second transformation in Bombay. If you are a successful and handsome young man wanting to score with every girl you meet, your reputation spreads. A perverse fascination kicked in and Shyam never starved for girls thereafter. He became a serial philanderer. Still, there was a longing for her. Many years later, a friend asked him if he was happy. It touched a raw nerve, painfully reminding him of Shwe.

Shyam did not respond to his friend. But the question led him to introspect—must temporary highs be a permanent pursuit? Once he even considered changing his lifestyle. But there were too many temptations and the flesh was weak, so he succumbed readily. Like a honeybee, he kept flitting from one flower to the other.

Now, in the mild autumn of his life, he admitted to us that evening that he was an old roué; a harmless, handsome remnant of a man whose greatest pleasures in life were girls and booze.

His flesh had begun to sag under his cheeks, and he checked the path ahead before taking the next step. He continued to look forward to his daily tipple, but it was no longer hard liquor—his preferred drink was now a glass of wine. His attitude towards women had also changed; the setting sun no longer excited in him the prospect of another long pleasurable night. Rather, he found himself wondering why the nights were so long. Women still found him good company, but only as a harmless, slightly irreverent lunchtime companion.

But there was still hope. There would still be a glint in Shyam's eyes when he would see a pretty girl; his spirit would goad him to make the effort and pursue her. He would rise then to try his luck one more time.

twenty

That was Shyam's story. I wondered if I envied the two brothers for their womanizing ways. Honestly, I was not so sure. I had not been adventurous, no one had ever advised me to enjoy an affair. Even if someone had said so, I would not have paid any attention, because mine was an obsessive love.

There were other differences as well. I was not athletic like the brothers. Nor was I of a sunny disposition like them. In fact, I was a bit of a loner. Since we had been sitting for hours, I wanted to stretch my legs. So I got up, alarming Shiv.

'Don't go!' he protested.

'I'm not going anywhere. I need to exercise.'

I took two quick rounds of the garden, breathing long and deep to fill my lungs with fresh air. Those two rounds of the garden helped clear whatever little confusion there was in my head. I was ready for more malt. In this fresh frame of mind, I wished I was young again—young enough to sing and dance.

In my youth, I had not been the master of my heart because I had been in love with Sati. Even after so many years, that glow had not dimmed and I would find myself thinking of her every so often.

The first time I met Sati was the very first time I saw her. It does not often happen like that, or at least that was not the way boys met girls back then. We were more conservative and far too tentative. The fear of rejection held us back.

Exactly a month after we joined college, a few of us had bunked class to go to the college cafe for chai and some gup-shup, or adda, as a Bengali friend put it. I remember that day well. It was mid-July, when it is monsoon season in Delhi, and the weather was playing funny tricks. It would rain furiously for an hour, clogging up the drains and flooding roads. Then, all of a sudden, the sun would break out of the clouds as if to dry up the excess water and muck from the roads. It was one of those days when a stray ray of the sun would catch an unsuspecting raindrop on a young grass blade to produce a rainbow.

I saw her then.

Let me say that, for a moment, everyone in the cafe froze, all conversation stopped, and I kept looking at her in awe. One of my friends whispered, 'That's rude, don't be so direct.' But I was beyond caring. I was not going to be like one of the many who camouflaged their intense interest in sideway glances.

Sati walked into the cafe regally, as if she owned the place. Unlike other girls who wore jeans to college, she was dressed simply but elegantly in a cotton salwar kameez. "Modern" is a state of mind,' she told me later, explaining her choice of clothes.

There were two of them and they chose a table in a far corner, away from the noisy part of the cafe. Once they were seated, I got up impulsively and walked over to their table, surprising them.

'Hi,' I said boldly. But truth be told, I did not have a follow-up line with me.

'Hi,' Sati said in mild surprise.

'May I sit down?' I asked rashly.

Sati's friend, the one who I had not acknowledged so far, said, 'Sit down.' Then, she added with a twinkle in her eye, 'Tell us about all the bad things you do.'

What I did next might seem very mushy now, but at that time my friends thought I had acted smart. I looked into Sati's eyes and said, 'I am nothing but a humble admirer.'

The rest, as they say, was history. From that day onwards, Sat-Sati became an item. We were inseparable.

Walking that night in the garden, I also began to think of the time when Sati had strolled in the same garden with Mrs Keeling. I had been there as well, but I had been content to see them bond. Therefore, I had been happy walking a few steps behind them. It was discreet enough to give them space, yet, I was within hearing range.

As usual, Sati did most of the talking. She would be having the most ordinary conversation with her friends and all of a sudden she would say something profound. Something similar happened in the middle of her conversation with Mrs Keeling.

'I came to Mussoorie to escape desire,' Sati said, surprising Mrs Keeling. A sentence like that would awe the chai-and-samosa crowd in a college canteen. But Mrs Keeling stopped in the middle of the garden. She turned around to face Sati, held her by the arm, and said, 'Say that again.'

When Sati repeated the words, she asked, 'Why should you escape desire? That is a negative emotion. You are young, you must celebrate every moment of your youth. And desire, my dear, is a very precious part of it. You should not reject it.'

'But I must renounce the desire to enjoy it.'

'That's a contradiction.,' Mrs Keeling said, conviction ringing in her firm voice. 'Love does not mean giving up. It means giving.'

'Come, give me your hand,' Mrs Keeling demanded.

Sati extended her hand obediently. Mrs Keeling held it for a moment, admiring her long artistic fingers. Cupping the fingers of Sati's right hand over her palm, Mrs Keeling said, 'Squeeze it. Squeeze your hand hard so you can capture all the air you want inside it.'

Sati squeezed until the knuckles of her hand began to hurt. By then, all the air had escaped from her closed fist. Was it for this that Mrs Keeling had asked her to clench hard?

'Now open it,' Mrs Keeling asked.

Sati did as she was told.

'Now you have all the air you could want, right in your palm! Isn't that so?' Mrs Keeling asked.

Sati nodded.

'It is the same with life,' Mrs Keeling continued. 'If you apply pressure and renounce, you are the loser. Giving up is not the right way, giving is.'

'In love?'

'Yes, in love too. Giving enhances love.'

'But I want to contribute to the world. I want to help

orphans, and maybe, even teach children.'

'How can you contribute to society if you are dissatisfied yourself? There is a time and a place for everything in life. This is the time for love, for fulfilling your desire. The world can wait.'

Sati nodded again, looking into Mrs Keeling's smoke-grey eyes. The alertness in those eyes was in contrast to the crow's feet around them. Seeing her eyes and sharp facial features, Sati was convinced that, in her youth, Mrs Keeling must have been very pretty, in a porcelain fragile way. With time, her beauty had been overwhelmed by the lines that now creased her face. Still, she lit up hearts with her optimism.

'Look at me,' Mrs Keeling said. 'Do I have even a single negative emotion? Life is too wonderful to waste on negative quibbles.'

'Yes,' Sati said with a spring in her step.

Then, they had moved away from me for a couple of brisk rounds of the garden. Their voices had trailed off to merge with laughter.

I smiled as I thought of their merry tones. They must have had the same view of the garden that I was witnessing now as I walked up and down its length. One side of the garden led to a dead end because Mrs Keeling's bungalow stood at the furthest end of the town. A steep rock acted as the final boundary for the bungalow and Mussoorie. To the right side of the garden, there was a sheer drop, leading to a wooded valley. On the other side, parallel to it, ran the driveway. It was separated by a boundary wall from the main road. The other end of the garden, closer to where we were sitting, overlooked a boarding school.

Due to its remote location, the bungalow was undisturbed by city noises. Some school buses came by in the morning, otherwise there was hardly any traffic on that road.

The only regular source of noise around Mrs Keeling's bungalow were the schoolchildren. We looked forward to hearing their boisterous shouts when they played in the school ground. Except for that, it was quiet through the day, unless a bird flew overhead and chirped mid-flight.

'Haven't you had enough exercise?' Shiv yelled impatiently.

I was about to return to the table, but I changed my mind after hearing his command. 'One last round,' I said busily and walked on.

$\mathcal{I}$ t would be fair to say that I took fiendish delight in offending Shiv. This feeling was mutual, but I had successfully disguised my emotions, until recently. This change to open hostility took place the day after we saw the computer declaration, making me Mrs Keeling's favourite son.

Shiv had assumed all along that he was Mrs Keeling's favourite, much ahead of Shyam. I was nowhere in the picture. That was why his face was drained of colour upon reading her declaration in my favour. Shyam, too, may have been surprised, but I didn't think he bore any ill will towards me.

Slightly after seeing Mrs Keeling's computer declaration, I had deliberately stepped out of the room for a bit. When I had returned unexpectedly early, I had overheard Shiv complaining to his older brother, 'What was the need for Ma to name him her favourite son? Didn't we matter to her?'

'She always treated him like us, a real son,' Shyam had replied, trying to calm him down.

'I don't think so,' Shiv had snapped. 'She took pity on him

because he was poor.'

'Don't be stupid,' Shyam had yelled at him.

Shiv's venom had shocked me. I thought he was worse than a snake because snakes do not go around pretending they are poison-free.

After reading Mrs Keeling's declaration, and on seeing Shiv's reaction to it, I had become openly hostile to Shiv. I would take great delight in rattling him. Like now, when I was deliberately prolonging a third round of walking in the garden just to add to his exasperation.

Finally, as I was about to sit down, he asked, 'Are you sure you do not want to do pee-pee?'

'Good you reminded me.'

Shiv cursed me sotto voce, but it was loud enough for all of us to hear. I laughed and went to the bathroom.

Shiv tugged at his shawl and sat up in his chair when I returned. He was expecting that I would now, at long last, start off. But I asked instead, 'Do you know what?'

'What is it now?' Shiv screamed, shaking a fist at me.

'Some of the best thoughts come to me when I am peeing.'

'And what happens when you do the other thing?' Shyam could not resist the jibe.

Before I could respond to that trick question, Shiv asked, 'What was the great thought this time?'

This was one more of Shiv's irritating habits . He would not let the other person finish; he had to butt in. There was a time when his interruptions irritated us. But over the years, Shyam and I had learned to ignore them. We would wait for him to finish, and then we would simply carry on. So, I kept my cool and said, 'While I was peeing, I figured out why I am such a gifted storyteller.'

'Oh,' Shyam punctuated quizzically.

I never took offence at Shyam's interruptions because there was no question of any spite. In fact, Shyam had hardly ever spoken disparagingly about anyone. Therefore, I carried on, 'Heat is of the essence. It is the trigger for my tales. Heat reminds me of the days immediately after the Partition of India.'

I told them how I remembered every detail of those days like it was carved on my heart. Sitting around the tandoor, sweltering in its heat, I would hear tales of people being slaughtered by swords, daggers, and knives during the exodus from what became Pakistan. People also narrated tragic accounts of loot, hunger, thirst and sickness. Listening to people tell their stories must have lit the creative spark in me.

There were gory descriptions of men turning into beasts, of trainloads of dead bodies arriving at railway stations. Every day, people exchanged new stories and spoke of new horrors. It seemed as if blood would never stop flowing. Partition was a time of monumental public angst. To this day, my mental association with the tandoor is one of sorrow, of tears mourning the loss of homes and the inherited way of life. 14 August 1947 was a cursed day for us. It made us refugees; exiles in our own land.

'We were fortunate,' Shyam said when I finished. 'Neither heat nor the Partition bothered us here in Mussoorie. Even the tales of horror reached us remotely through matter-of-fact and impersonal radio reports.'

'Partition ruptured every bond,' I whispered back.

'You people didn't try hard enough,' Shiv pontificated. He seemed secretly pleased at hearing the account of my suffering.

'What could we have done?' I asked, annoyed.

'You could have appealed to the authorities. You should have done something.'

I could sense that he was riling me on purpose. So, I said with as much calm as I was capable of, 'You go to a police station to report a rape, a kidnapping, or a murder. But where do you file a report for one million murders and millions of lost homes? No one knows how many women were raped or kidnapped. And even if there was a big enough police station to deal with these million cases, who could it act against? After Partition, an Indian police station had no jurisdiction in Pakistan. At the stroke of Nehru's midnight hour, all heinous acts were written off the criminal register by an arbitrary line called the border.'

'But must suffering be constant?' Shyam asked reflectively. 'Must that pain last forever?'

'I suppose it will, as long as our generation lives. Who knows what might happen afterwards!' I replied.

'The next generation will not carry the baggage of bitterness,' Shiv piped in.

'It must—there must be a reminder. It should act as a permanent warning of what happens when hate transcends hatred,' Shyam insisted, 'otherwise the same carnage will be repeated. Future generations should have a record of how suffocating that long, dark night was.'

Shyam was being sensitive to my concern. But I didn't want the evening to turn sombre, so, to lighten the mood, I told them, that in all the grimness of that time, there were moments of laughter. Adversity could not hold back the Punjabi spirit. I told them that I may not have comprehended all the dark tales or understood the occasional joke fully, but the sheer variety had made me a good teller of tales.

'We are impressed,' Shiv mocked. 'The next time we want a kid to grow up as a great storyteller, we will arrange another partition, and an extra hot tandoor.'

If Shyam had made this comment, I would not have given it a second thought. But it was Shiv, and I didn't trust him. Once I had overheard him tell a mutual friend that I had left Sati in the lurch and gone off to the US looking for other pastures. This remark had made me feel decadent and bereft of any sense of honour. Quite honestly, I had been disgusted with the way he had kept pursuing the issue. Had it been some other person, I would have given him a cold look and would never have spoken to him again.

The conversation slowly shifted to Sati and me, and he continued to talk as callously about it as before. I had a mild disposition, but I would get riled when he made rude remarks about my love for Sati. Sometimes I wondered why he did that. Was it jealousy or a case of latent infatuation? How could I describe to such a person what I had been through?

'The last thirty odd years have been terrible for both of us,' I said. 'I do not recall many happy moments. It was sadness that lingered as troubles came in waves. It was mostly depressing stuff, and while the world moved on, we were still there waiting for the next move.'

Shiv made what was meant to be a thoughtful face. 'How did you know she was suffering if you were not in touch with each other?' he asked.

'We talked of the past when we met,' I replied. 'I can only say that our life is now arranged in such a complicated way that I end up feeling bewildered no matter how I look at it. Sometimes, in my deep frustration, I have wondered if Sati is permanently unhappy with the world.'

'That can't be so,' Shyam said. 'You are being unfair to her.'

'Like me, Sati, too, is living life in the rewind mode, making it hellish for herself and for me,' I continued. 'All this while, I have longed for those carefree days in college when nothing else mattered except Sati and my thoughts about her. It has been such a long time since then. After all these years, her eyes still haunt me,' I said finally.

'Your passion confuses me,' Shyam interjected bluntly. 'If you pine for her, why don't the two of you get married?'

'It's not so simple,' I said sternly. 'You can marry if you can physically locate the other person. For a long time, I did not know where she was. When I went to Pune and asked her neighbours, they had no clue either.'

'How did you find her?' Shiv asked, impatiently.

'By sheer chance. I traced her in a girls' convent here in Mussoorie.'

'But why here?' Shyam asked. 'Mussoorie is small, it is just a village that expands into a little town in summers. She was a city girl.'

I shook my head in a manner which suggested that I neither agreed nor disagreed with him.

'That's Sati for you,' I said, measuring each word. 'She had always talked of going away one day to a place so far where no one would ever be able to find her.'

'But why?' Shyam wailed.

'She said she wanted to find her own space, but I never took her seriously, thinking of it as a passing fancy. It might have stayed that way but for my disappearance from the university. That was the trigger for her decision. She thought I had left without bothering to say goodbye to her because I wanted to break our relationship. Unfortunately, she did not know that I was in jail then.'

'Sometimes luck plays games even with its favourites,' Shyam remarked helpfully.

'How can you call us luck's favourites after hearing all this? We were scorned by fate.'

'Did she suspect something?' Shiv asked, probing again. His persistence irritated me, but I let it pass.

'No, never. That was never a factor. She had far too much faith in me to think that I could be two-timing her. What bothered her was my disappearance. It was followed quickly by her parents' death. That settled the issue. She was determined to get away from it all. That was how she ended up coming to Mussoorie, and that too, in its remotest part beyond Cloud's End. I got to know about it through a chance remark by a friend's

RAJIV DOGRA

daughter. She told me that every class that graduates out of her school is asked for one wish by the principal.'

'Oh!' both Shyam and Shiv whispered.

'For the last thirty years,' my friend's daughter said, 'every graduating class has come up with the same wish, that Sati should gift her eyes to the school.'

'Yet, her most ardent admirer could not look into those eyes,' Shyam whispered.

'For thirty long years,' I sighed.

'I did look into her eyes eventually,' I added. 'When I heard that Sati was teaching in a school here, I rushed to Mussoorie.'

'Oh, you did!' Shyam shrieked, jumping out of his chair with joy. 'You rascal, you found her and you didn't tell us anything in the last two days!'

Before I could tell him anything, Shiv interrupted us, 'The next time you meet her, you should quote from a poem by the Greek poet C. P. Cavafy:

You said: I'll go to another country, go to another shore,
find another city better than this one…

'That sounds good,' I said, interrupting him. Thas was enough for Shiv. He needed no further encouragement to complete the poem.

'Cavafy goes on to describe the futility of leaving the familiar for the unknown. These last lines of the poem are magical,' Shiv continued cheerfully.

You won't find a new country, won't find another shore.
This city will always pursue you.

You'll walk the same streets, grow old in the same neighbourhoods, turn grey in these same houses.
You'll always end up in this city. Don't hope for things elsewhere: there's no ship for you, there's no road...

It was a good poem, but why did Shiv want me to quote these dark lines to Sati? Did he really think that she would return to Delhi after hearing this poem? Unless, he wanted me to convey to her that it was he who had chosen this bit of poetry for her. Doubts like these made me wary of Shiv.

twenty-two

I had loved every moment of the time I had spent talking to Margaret in the plane that day. Or to put it precisely, it had been fascinating listening to her because she was doing most of the talking. But in the end, she had left me with a bruised ego. Was I so insignificant that she did not find it necessary to even ask my name? Would she have done the same had one of the two brothers been her fellow passenger? Perhaps not. In fact, I was reasonably certain that she would have asked for their name and telephone number as well.

You could put it down as envy, but I often made such comparisons. Shyam was definitely my favourite of the two brothers, and I did not make any great effort to hide the fact that I was partial to him. Sometimes, when Shiv hinted subtly at Shyam's flaws, I ignored him and his hints. On the other hand, my feelings towards Shiv were marked by ambivalence. It was difficult to say whether I resented his self-absorption or envied the fact that he was so good-looking. Perhaps this confusion of the good and the not-so good about him ended up confusing me.

In contrast, Shyam was an open book. He was modest, and he admitted readily that he was made of plain clay. 'I am an ordinary man who is trying to find his place in the mist called the world,' he would often say. 'I make no claim to heroism.'

I also liked the fact that he did not hedge. If you asked him a question, you got a straight answer. For example, when I asked him if parting with his partners had been painful, he replied honestly, 'It does hurt, after all it involves two human beings. Fortunately, there have been no ugly scenes so far, instead, there was always this understanding that if it came to parting ways, it would be done gracefully, without fuss.'

'Hey, Sat. Do you remember the big love of our lover boy?' Shyam asked, suddenly.

'What are you talking about?' Shiv protested.

'Your love life,' Shyam replied.

'My love life? Why mine? Why not Sat's love life? That should be more interesting,' Shiv protested.

They knew the story of my life and of my passion that longed for a life others took for granted. They also knew that in my present condition, I wanted nothing more than to be forgotten by people. It was all that I aspired to—to be left alone with my loneliness.

Shiv knew all that. That was why he was not aiming at my fictitious love life. And I don't think the prospect of his nascent love being put on display bothered him much either. Something else was worrying him.

In all likelihood, it had to do with Mrs Keeling's decision to anoint me as her favourite son. That must have hurt him deeply. As the younger, more pampered, and her 'real' son, he had assumed that he was the apple of her eye. But her dying declaration in my favour must have rankled him. His body language, and the way he sometimes ignored me on purpose, conveyed that I had usurped what was his by right.

I must clarify that this was only my impression because nothing was said to me directly. But sometimes the implied hurts more than a direct verbal assault.

Earlier, whenever I felt low, a remark by Mrs Keeling provided me succour. She would say, 'Remember the importance of forgetting if grief is not to become overwhelming.'

'We have been talking continuously about women. We should talk a bit about Ma,' Shiv said unexpectedly.

'Ma would want us to talk about the good times,' Shyam asserted with a magisterial sweep of his hands. 'Actually, she may have enjoyed ribbing you.' Then, he turned sombre and added, 'If she was alive she would have ribbed you about your first love,' Shyam repeated, 'that is, if she was alive.' His eyes misted over as he added that final bit.

Shiv shifted uncomfortably in his seat. 'What is this thing about my first love? Doesn't everyone have a first love? You've got to start off somewhere,' Shiv said lamely.

'Your first love is always unique. It haunts you all your life,' Shyam said smoothly.

Shyam was right. The most cherished moment of my love for Sati was the first time I saw her. That opening image has remained etched in my mind since then. When I would be down emotionally, I would close my eyes and think of that first sight.

It was soothing.

But Shiv was different. He was so self-absorbed that he rarely had time for flashbacks about others. But Shyam didn't hesitate taking him on, and there were questions bubbling in his mind. He started with the most harmless one. 'You have not named any of your first love interests.'

'Why do you want to know their names?' Shiv asked suspiciously.

'Just curious, nothing else.'

For a moment, Shiv seemed to be wavering, as if age and memory had combined to soften him. But then, he took a deep breath and said firmly, 'No, I cannot tell you their names. That would be defiling their memory. Names are unimportant anyway.'

'Oh.'

'Names are given to goods like soaps and biscuits to help people make a choice. Should they take a Lux or a Rexona?' Shiv carried on, 'But where is the question of choice in love? You don't go to a supermarket to pick up your love interest from the many items on a shelf. Love is special, it is pure. It must always remain nameless.'

This is how conversations tended to be with Shiv. He heard you out, you were allowed to express an opinion, but thereafter, it was like talking to a wall. He had a final view on everything.

'You never married,' once a friend asked in a matter-of-fact fashion without putting any great passion into his enquiry, 'Given a chance would you have married?'

'Why? Why should I marry? Where is the need?'

'I just asked,' his friend said defensively.

'I wouldn't marry even if someone were to turn the clock back to make me a twenty year old again. Marriage makes you bitter and desiccated. Being alone keeps you lively and warm.'

'I come from a different god,' Shiv's friend confessed amiably. 'My obstacles are many and my path has numerous thorns. I need a companion to help me along. For me, it is difficult being loveless. What about you? Have you ever been loveless?'

This wasn't the first time Shiv had heard an argument in favour of marriage. It wasn't the first time either that he was going to demolish it with a counter-point of his own. But this was certainly the first time that the message had been delivered so artfully.

'I am in a perpetual state of love. In fact, there is so much love around me that I have transcended love. I am beyond love,' Shiv reached for a glass of water before carrying on with his thesis. 'You might now ask me how I express my love in such a state. Well, my answer is simple. When you are beyond love, what is the need for expression? And if sometimes you must convey your feelings, then what is the need for words?'

'I don't believe this,' Shyam said, rolling with laughter.

Shyam was like that. He could be talking about a serious issue one moment, and the very next, he would effortlessly slip into the most frivolous mode. Shyam hated thinking about the future. It was enough for him that he had gone through the day on his terms; tomorrow belonged to the unknown, a part of unknown and unwanted ambition.

'You mean all this actually happened when you were there?'

Shyam was referring to the conversation between Shiv and his friend, which I had happened to overhear.

'I'm not making it up,' I replied.

'That's not the point. The issue is that you were there and yet did not utter a word. I find that hard to believe.'

'I was the fly on the wall. How could I speak?'

Still, that conversation had set me thinking. I had known Shiv for a long time and if there was one thing I was certain of in life, it was that he would never marry. But that did not make him stone-hearted. In the thirty years or so that I had known him, I had always sensed in him a longing, even a feeling of having missed out on lasting love.

Once Mrs Keeling was pressing him to get married in the way all mothers anxiously do. 'How can I?' Shiv resisted. 'I must trust someone to marry her.' And to confound her further, he added, 'How can I love if I don't trust?'

'Don't confuse me with big words. Let me tell you that you are getting old,' Mrs Keeling admonished. 'Remember, time has two dimensions. Its passage is determined by the rhythm of sun, its depth by the rhythm of passion. Just one glance suffices. But for that, you must let yourself go. You are preventing yourself from falling in love.'

As usual, Mrs Keeling was right; if you desire something with intensity, you always get it.

To be fair to Shiv, I felt his failed love affairs still hurt him. I also knew Shiv well enough to realize when he was being luminous just for effect.

It was true that he was ambitious; he would push through

a crowd of high achievers to emerge smiling. But there was another side to him that was more complicated. He would make a constant effort at being pleasant. It was a part of his perpetual effort at camouflage.

Despite his social act, he liked to be alone at the end of the day. Some great melancholy would begin to haunt him then. He would never admit it to anyone, not even to Shyam or me, but I had a feeling that in the stillness of a dark, lonely night, he would wonder if he had done the right thing by staying single. That was why I felt that his bravado was an act, a front to leave people guessing.

Sometimes, I had this urge to tell him to get married. But I would hold back, after all, there wasn't much that I could say on a complex issue like marriage.

'He will not marry. I agree with you there,' Shyam said, 'whether he should marry is not for us to decide. But one thing I am sure about, and it is this—there is some Italian blood in his English veins.'

Shiv was listening carefully, but he did not react to his brother's statement. He did not even ask for the source of Shyam's information. His silence conveyed that Shyam had a point.

However, I could not restrain myself. 'Really?' I wondered.

'He has to have Italian blood because he loves feta and olives,' Shyam replied.

All three of us laughed. It was true that Shiv was fond of Italian food, but so were many others. It didn't make them Italian.

'Look at the physical evidence,' Shyam continued. 'Like an

Italian man, he is a compulsive flirt. He flirts as naturally as other men breathe.'

'Most men flirt,' I insisted.

'They can't flirt as smoothly as an Italian stallion,' Shyam elaborated. 'Like an Italian lover, Shiv pays attention to detail. He will look deep into a girl's eyes as if those are the most beautiful pair he has ever seen in his life, and he will open the door for her. He makes a woman feel like a princess with every look. And he breathes passion with his warm breath. It is difficult to resist such a man.'

That bit about Shiv looking into a girl's eyes as if they were the most beautiful pair got me worried because I had often seen him look for long into Sati's eyes.

Suspicion like this was hard to live with—angst bubbled loudly and tearfully to the surface every so often. I had often wanted to ask Shiv, 'Tell me, why are you so interested in Sati?' But I would keep dithering, and by the time I would decide to ask, I would be too late.

Meanwhile, Shiv was laughing at what Shyam had said. His laughter came in short spurts, like a car engine that seemed to be, but never actually was, stalled. It was the sort of unnatural laugh where your embarrassment makes you put on a happy face.

---

twenty-three

*A*ppearance-wise, Shyam was not in the same league as Shiv. For one, he was not as handsome as Shiv. In fact, he had one of the biggest faces mounted on a human body. But it was not a frightening sight because he was large enough to pull it off.

When he was young, Shyam was built like a wrestler and he would take care to nurture his body. By the final year of college, he had become large enough for people to be wary of him. But he never used his largeness to overwhelm others, not even when he contested successfully to become the president of the university's student union.

'When you are with the other young people, you must use charm, not aggression,' he used to tell his friends in the university. 'You have to have the right instincts when judging others and you should learn to use your personality as a weapon. The important thing is to calm people down.'

He never forgot this dictum himself.

Wherever he was, whatever the circumstance, he kept a level head and a sharp eye. He also developed an instinct for reading others' body language, of being able to spot the vulnerabilities in others. He did not use this power as a weapon of blackmail, but only to get the better of his opposition.

To sum up the contrast between the two brothers, it would be fair to say that he did not have the presence that Shiv commanded with his sharp features and Greek-god look.

Shyam was more English, always proper and well turned out with polished shoes. When it rained, he wore a bowler hat and carried a black umbrella—this completed the picture of his Englishness. Nothing was ever out of place with him. But he lacked the spontaneous charm of his brother, and his magnetism. He lacked Shiv's quick wit and his razor-sharp intellect. Shyam was too much of a 'nice guy'.

'I am no cat,' Shyam admitted. 'I'm more likely to be held up by a bandit.'

'A bandit? What happened with the bandit?' Shiv asked excitedly. Suddenly, he was alert; the previous droopy look had been replaced by wide-open eyes and upturned ears. He was now watching Shyam like a hawk.

But this was one chapter of his life that Shyam did not wish to talk about.

Unlike Shiv, he regarded true love as a precious gift that could not be shared. It had to remain a sacred bond between two individuals, beyond conditions and without red lines. But the secret had slipped out and Shyam realized too late that he had himself blocked the escape route.

'If Shyam was held up by a bandit it had to be female. Tell me what happened, Sat.'

Shiv assumed that I would be in on all of Shyam's secrets. So, his query was directed at me, but I looked away. How could I let out Shyam's secret without his approval?

'What happened with the bandit?' Shiv asked Shyam this time. 'You never told me this.'

'Ask Sat,' Shyam said. 'He knows.'

'Sat never listens to me,' Shiv responded petulantly. 'You ask him to tell me. He's your friend.'

'Friend? What do you mean friend? Sat is not a friend, he is a brother,' Shyam snapped.

I knew the story but my telling it would have infuriated Shiv further. The two of us were already going through a rough patch and I did not want to make it worse. Therefore, as I leaned forward to refill my glass, I whispered to Shyam asking him to tell his story.

'Narration is more important than the narrator,' Shyam insisted. 'You do it. You give the right sense of drama.'

This is how I ended up telling the story of Shyam and the bandit.

twenty-four

Shyam

The bandit emerged out of thin air to block his way. 'Give me your money,' she demanded.

Shyam was intent on getting to the bank quickly; therefore, he was huffing ahead with his head down. In that rush, her words came to him in a jumbled mish-mash, but it was enough to make him look up. He was struck immediately by the superior quality of her coat. 'It must have cost a lot,' he thought.

'Give me your money,' she repeated menacingly.

She was too pretty to be a bandit and rather fragile physically to be anything more than a harmless nuisance. But when he looked down, he noticed the bulge in her coat pocket where her hidden hand was aiming a pistol at him.

'Money,' she hissed again, shaking the pistol.

'I've only a few pounds,' Shyam replied, patting his trouser pockets as proof.

'No problem,' she bristled, 'I can show you the way to the bank.'

She was showing the classic signs of someone new at her work, her impatience reflecting a lack of confidence. Obviously she was nervous, and for a moment, he toyed with the idea of taking her on.

Shyam was a black belt in karate; on a good day, he could take on two strong men in combat. The bandit was frail and he could have hit her hard, if he wanted to. The other alternative was to turn and run away. There was no way she could have caught up with him. But he rejected both options. It was morally impossible for him to hit a woman, even if she was a bandit. And on a practical note, her gun worried him; he couldn't outrun a bullet. Considering the impossible odds against a speeding bullet, Shyam decided to walk with her to the bank.

'How much do you want?' he asked gruffly in the crowded bank.

She did not respond. Instead, she was casing a joint, one hand on the hip and the other holding the gun. Hers was a languid pose, like that of the tobacco-chewing cowboys before the shootout starts in the movies. But it was a carefully controlled casualness, as with a spring before it uncoils. In fact, she was doing more than that, she was multitasking. Besides being ready to draw her gun, she was busily looking around for potential threats.

Shyam, too, was glancing about anxiously. Apart from customers, there were a number of bank employees milling around and there was an alert-looking security guard as well.

For a brief moment, he was tempted to shout for help and simultaneously run to hide behind a pillar. But in the end, he decided against it.

The idea that he was being held up by a good-looking woman was darkly romantic, and truth be told, Shyam was beginning to find her more ravishing with every passing minute.

'How much?' Shyam asked again.

'A hundred pounds,' she demanded.

'A hundred!' Shyam was taken aback by the modest size of the ransom.

'A hundred,' she echoed.

'I could have given you that much straightaway. What was the need to walk all the way to the bank?'

'Go to the cash desk and withdraw a hundred pounds,' she said sternly. 'Do it now.'

When he handed over two fifty-pound notes to her, she pointed the gun again at him again and said, 'Follow me.'

It was a weird hold up, and it was getting weirder by the minute. First, she wanted a ridiculously low sum of money, and then, instead of keeping him in the shooting sight of her gun, she asked Shyam to follow her.

But he wasn't behaving in a better way either.

She had given him the perfect chance to escape. Instead of following her, he could have steadily increased the distance between them before finally slipping away. But he was faithfully following her to an undisclosed destination and further risks.

Since Shyam was walking behind her, he could now see her properly—the petite hips of a young girl and the confident gait of a sprinter. It was then that he noticed a contradiction. Her well-groomed, shiny long hair could not have been kept in their silky condition in the dust and rigour of a grab life of a bandit. Moreover, she was wearing expensive clothes—the type which could not have been bought on small change, like a hundred pounds.

Shyam was so fully absorbed in observing every little detail of the hold-up artist that he had lost all sense of direction and any idea of where they were going. He was taken aback when she finally led him into a restaurant.

'Why is she taking me there?' he wondered. 'Why this café?' Shyam could not resist asking her when they were seated inside.

'Thieves have a value system.'

Since she had taken off her coat before slipping into her chair, he was watching carefully to see where she had hidden the gun. She shook her fist at him and laughed. 'This was the gun. My fist and the forefinger were the bulge of a gun for you.'

'Surely you don't need money?' Shyam asked.

'It is not about money.'

If it was not about money—and that was easy to believe because a hundred pounds was too insignificant an amount for a woman with expensive tastes—why had she taken such a huge risk? The entire thing was becoming more mysterious by the minute. The way things were unfolding, Shyam almost expected her to return his hundred pounds.

'The hundred pounds stay with me,' she said, reading him.

When the bill came, she insisted on paying for the coffee and cakes. As she took out her purse, he noticed it bulging with fifty-pound notes.

'Were there so many today?' Shyam asked.

'You were the first,' she said, looking at him slyly. Then, pointing at her purse, she said, 'This is my hard-earned money.'

'Hard-earned money?' Shyam repeated softly.

'This robbing business is a diversion.'

'But why?'

She began to explain her complex philosophy. 'Once I watched a smart-looking lady get up at a riverfront with a satisfied look. The source of her happiness was the fishing net which contained a large fish that she must have caught. On the way back home, she stopped for a moment to go to the toilet. When she came out to pick up her things again, the fish was gone!

'The smart lady looked all around except in the direction of the grinning cat who was sitting by the side of the toilet with the fish in her mouth. I was amused by that incident but it was the cat who inspired me; she showed me the possibility of enjoying the fruit of someone else's hard work. It was a cunning demonstration of the survival of the fittest.'

It was just about an hour from the time she had first accosted Shyam with that fake gun, but already, he was beginning to appreciate the fact that she was a seductive speaker.

After explaining her complex philosophy, she turned in her seat and bent down sideways. With a shake of her head, she spread her hair like a giant fan behind her. Then, languidly, she weaved the fingers of her right hand through her hair and began to caress the strands in a slow, deliberate fashion.

Shyam's heart was not calm any longer. He began to pine for her from the time he saw her caress her hair so enticingly. From that moment he found himself hovering between lust and self-denial.

Shyam was not impulsive by nature. Usually, he would deliberate and take his time before making the next move. But in one rash moment he reached over the table and placed his hand over hers. She flinched a little, but she did not disengage. Her soft hand stayed under his. Shyam took it as a sign that maybe the feeling was mutual; that she too was smitten.

'The root of all complexities is loneliness,' she said, sliding her hand away at last. She smiled mysteriously and picked up her cup of coffee to gaze at the grainy coffee remains at the bottom for signs of future tidings.

True to her unexpected twists and turns, she sparkled suddenly, 'Say hi to forever.'

'Yes,' Shyam responded weakly. But truly speaking, he didn't know what she meant by that.

Then, looking directly into his eyes, she asked, 'Do you want to join me in my solitude?'

'Wasn't that a little forward, even for a bandit?' Shyam wondered, sensing danger.

It was true that after the separation from his last girlfriend, he was looking for excitement, but hooking up with this girl was an invitation to wild adventure. It was reckless to decide on the spot, and rather uncharacteristically, he said to himself, 'To hell with the consequences!'

Without bothering to find out her name, he said, 'It might

be a rollicking ride; but why not, why the hell not!'

■

Since they had agreed to pair up, Shyam thought it was time they got to know each other better. 'Why do you rob?' he asked.

'For fun,' she said simply.

'But that's dangerous. You could end up in a jail.'

'People snort cocaine for a high. Isn't that dangerous?'

'I suppose you have a point there.'

Then, he got up formally, extended his right hand, and said, 'Hi, I'm Shyam.'

'From India!' she bellowed in a voice loud enough for the entire restaurant to hear, 'How exotic. I have never had an Indian lover before.'

'And you are?'

'I'm Italian. Italiano.'

'Nice. But your name?'

'Lara. Like Lara's theme, you know,' she said, fluttering her big eyes.

The name sounded more Slavic than Italian. But she was quick to clarify that her mother was American, and hence the name. This new bit of information about her mixed parentage kept Shyam guessing as to which side, the American or the Italian, was responsible for her reckless streak.

'They are both bohemian,' Lara clarified, anticipating his next question.

Her ability to read Shyam's mind could not be put down to intuition or telepathy. It was almost a craft; he would be thinking of something—the idea would just begin to take shape in his mind—and she would already know. These qualities took his admiration for her to a higher level.

The next five months were filled with fun and risk. Lara never revealed to him the nature of her regular job, but she kept busy five days a week for a good ten to twelve hours each day. Her chic formal clothes hinted that she was an executive of some sort. Her snappish, generally busy responses to telephone calls suggested that she had a lot on her plate.

She was also full of strange quirks. For example, she insisted Shyam to not call her by her name. 'It must be an anonymous relationship,' she asserted.

'How can it be anonymous? Your neighbours see me every day.'

'That can't be avoided. But you must not take my name unless it's an emergency.'

This was a quixotic restriction and Shyam tried one last time, 'If I can't take your name, how should I communicate?'

'That's not a problem,' she said. 'You can touch me to draw attention, or say hey, hi, hello, listen, or any of the many little things. But it must be impersonal; no names and that is something I insist upon.'

Like this, she had many funny rules.

Sometimes it irritated Shyam to put up with an eccentric person like her. But she was heart-achingly pretty and he was hopelessly smitten. She only had to look at him through the corner of her eyes to make him forget where he was.

Had she wanted, he was ready to say, 'Hi forever.'

One late evening, they were lying in bed when she said wistfully, 'When I die...'

'Shh, don't say that,' Shyam reached across to put his finger over her lips.

'Tell me, will you have a new girl when I die?'

'You want to come back all the way from up there to check if I have a new girlfriend? That's crazy.'

'If it was possible, and if I could come back,' she said dreamily, 'then the cool breeze that you would feel on your forehead on a summer evening like this would be my breath.'

Her eyes had misted over, and she began to look vacantly into the distant space—a sign of some great inner turmoil. Perhaps she was struggling about what and how much to share with him. Over the last few months, he had observed her moods and facial expressions so well that he could easily tell what was going on in her mind. A flash passed across her face, her body relaxed, giving the signal that she had made up her mind.

Then she narrated the story of her college life.

'We were a close-knit group, as many such college friendships are. There were eight of us—four boys and four girls. Each pair was deeply committed with vows of everlasting fidelity. It was idyllic and idealistic, almost too good to last forever. Since we were all from a reasonably upper middle class background, it was fashionable for us to be firebrand radicals. We shared some other passions of the age; Marx-Lenin during the day, and hashish in the evening.

'One day, without telling any of the girls, the four boys disappeared. You can imagine our condition and what we must have gone through. Six full months passed without any information about them. Then, one day, one of the boys returned. He told us tall tales of the crimes they had committed and how the four of them had engaged a large force of policemen; not just once but many times. Finally, he had been caught. The other three were on the run after killing a police officer.

'This friend spun for us many accounts of his heroism, of how he never broke down despite sustained police torture. But we learned later that he was the rat in the group; to save his skin, he had volunteered to tell all. It was on the basis of the information given by this friend that the police were able to track the others down. But instead of capturing them, the police shot each one of them in the back. This friend was pardoned and released by the police, but he never met us again. After that, the other three girls got married.'

'You never married?' Shyam asked.

"I heard the beat of an anguished drum. I am not a dark person, but I remain bitter to this day,' she said slowly. 'Try as I might, I can't come to terms with the injustice of what happened to our three friends.'

'You remain a practising Marxist-Leninist?'

'I suppose I am, at heart.'

She didn't have the physical wherewithal of the gun-toting cadre who disappear once every few weeks into the deep jungle for yet another operation. Obviously, hers was a conviction of intellectual variety.

'I don't blow up railway tracks or sabotage power stations,' Lara clarified, 'nor do I disappear deep into jungles. It is simply not an option for me. I cannot do that and hope to keep my job. But anger continues to rage in me against the inequities of society. I have still not been able to reconcile myself to the betrayal and murder of our friends. So, I let off that steam by occasionally robbing a rich man like you.'

'What have the rich done to you personally? They didn't kill your friends.'

'The rich corrupt everyone. They kill others by depriving them financially. Robbing them is my protest against their world. It is also my occasional revenge against the system which killed three of my friends. This is how I get back at the police, by breaking their law and by daring them. It is also my way of keeping my skills honed.'

'What do you do with the money?' Shyam asked.

'I give it to the first poor person I see.'

This account kept haunting Shyam over the next few days; he kept thinking obsessively about that fourth friend who had returned to tell them the story. The other thing that bothered him was her sense of guilt. The other three girls had got married but why was she continuing with her penance?

Finally, Shyam asked her about this friend.

'I don't know. I haven't kept in touch,' she responded in a rush. She took a deep breath to calm herself before adding, 'Once a common friend told me that he had adjusted well into his family's business.'

Shyam was going to leave it at that, but as an afterthought, he asked, 'Incidentally, who among the four of you was his girlfriend? She must have felt most hurt by what happened.'

'Yes.'

Then, drilling holes into the ground with her eyes, she added, 'It hurts. It still does.'

∎

'Good, now let's turn profound,' Shiv said.

'What did he mean by profound?' I wondered. Did he mean that the bandit affair was profane? Had Shyam made this remark, I would have taken it at its face value as a prankish one-liner. With Shiv, it was different. It was impossible to tell what was really going on in his mind.

But there was no point in fighting psychological battles with Shiv. He could be prickly without reason or conveniently thick-skinned when he wanted to be. He could cleverly deflect conversation and say that he did not mean to criticize Shyam, but merely meant it as a complement to me when he said, 'Let's turn profound.' There was simply no way one could get the better of Shiv.

Therefore, I pretended I had not heard his remark. Instead, I got back to telling them about Sati and me.

twenty-five

Sat

Our first meeting after thirty years was at the tea shop outside the school she was teaching in. I had reached the place first, so I saw her walk towards me. She looked almost the same as she did in our university days, neither plump, nor thin. The elegance in her steps, the confident flick of her head to put her loose hair back in place was just like before. Even the colour of her clothes was the same—a light pastel pink. It had to be pink because that was her favourite colour. The only difference was that instead of the youthful salwar kameez, she was now wearing a saree.

My memory of her was still fresh, unscathed by time. I knew exactly how she would react on seeing me. She would open her mouth and eyes wide in surprise, and then, for no reason at all, she would brush an imaginary lock of hair off her forehead.

During our time in college, I would sit awestruck in my

chair when she would come into the canteen for our meeting. My eyes would remain focused on her, watching every step she took. That was many summers ago. Since then, my dreams had been mocked to death by time.

I was no longer sure of the state of our relationship, so I stood up formally. I looked at her, and in that instant, I knew as clearly as there was life in me, that I loved her more than anything in the world. If I could summon the courage, I would have told her right then that all these years I had only thought of her. I also wanted to tell her that her image was a constant presence, it pursued me wherever I went and in whatever I did. But I hesitated.

When we were standing close together, we shook hands tentatively. Then we took our seats at a table by the window. That way, we had a clear view of the valley below, and we could avoid looking at the other customers.

I had saved so many questions to ask her. I had repeated them mentally as if perfecting them. In all these years, had she thought of me? Had she known where I was?

Most of all, I wanted to ask, 'Tell me, what have you done all these years? Tell me everything.'

But I did not ask these questions.

I did not want to flood her with my questions, nor did I wish to say anything even remotely insensitive. It was, therefore, awkward in the beginning because there were so many silences to be broken.

'Stylish,' I said finally, complimenting her look.

Sati smiled shyly.

'Where do you live?' I asked, after we had placed our order.

'Oh here, among the girls,' she said, waving her hand towards the school. 'I have a room. It is large, but simple, with a valley view, like the one we have here. It has white walls, but there is a blue trim around the windows.'

The waiter came with our order—a plate of piping hot pakoras and two cups of steaming tea. We reached simultaneously for the pakora plate and our hands touched, producing the same electricity as before.

'It is my fault really,' I said, conveying many meanings in that single sentence. 'I delay things.'

'No, not really,' Sati said, stirring her spoon slowly in the cup. 'I still like my tea lukewarm.'

'Distance was the villain.'

'I am waiting at the same crossroads,' Sati whispered, as if she was carrying on a conversation with the slow-moving spoon. 'You took a turn away from there.'

'Do you think I have lived in peace?' I protested.

'Must we fiddle with the truth?'

I tried to persuade her that it happened because she had gone away to Pune. But she was adamant that I had taken that first fateful step. Finally, the misunderstanding was cleared, and then we both cried. We stopped only when we ran out of tears. By then, it was getting dark outside.

'Shall we go for a walk?' Sati asked.

'Frankly, no,' I replied, 'it is quite nice here. And the view is good.'

The room was warm with a fire burning and I quite liked the

sound of wood crackling at regular intervals. It was comfortable in the room. Sati understood why I was being lazy, so she let it pass. But, as we finished our tea, she pressed again, 'It is quite remarkable down there,' she said, pointing at the play of shadow and light among the trees.

'Lead the way,' I said, getting up.

The path she chose took us through a patch of thin woodland. At times, it was unsteady to walk on because there was a thick padding of the uncleared leaves from the previous year. After we had walked for a bit, she said as much to me as to herself, 'I wish I could write.'

'What's the need?' I asked.

'Why, why shouldn't I write?' she countered.

'Writers write to create beauty,' I said. 'What in the world can be more beautiful than you?'

On a sudden impulse, I circled her slim waist with my hands, like a bracelet.

'They must be watching,' she said, pointing at the school, as she slipped out of my grasp.

Back in the tea shop, we sat silently, side by side, looking at the green, fertile valley. The dark shadows of the late evening began to cover the valley, gradually turning its vibrant green to dull grey. We remained mute spectators of this transformation, our thoughts frozen in that last day of college when hope had been alive.

■

'What happened then?' Shiv asked impatiently.

'It is strange that our first meeting after so many years should have taken place in a college-like setting again. I took it as a good omen.'

'Were you both tense because you were meeting after such a long time?' Shiv asked.

'No, except in the beginning and except for those initial questions, not at all,' I said spontaneously. 'No explanations were needed. There were no gaps to fill. We did not have to worry about how we sat or what we said; there was no need to pretend. It was such a nice and comfortable space to be in.'

'But still?' Shiv remarked.

'Yes, there was that. The "but still" had come up between us. When she spoke again, I thought she would say it was time to start a life together. But she surprised me by saying, "Let's meet when we can."'

Shiv and Shyam looked away tactfully when I wiped a tear.

'I tried to persuade her, I pleaded with her,' I continued in a half-choked voice, 'but she was resolute. She insisted that it had to be that way. She had found her peace. It did not mean that she did not love me any longer. As a matter of fact, she died a thousand deaths every day just thinking of me. But going back was impossible. Her fear of the world was greater than her love for me.'

'Did she mean "never" when she said no?' Shiv asked.

'It was tough in the beginning,' I replied. 'I thought if I longed for her with all my heart day after day, she might say yes eventually. So, I kept telling her every time we met that we should get married, that I would give up my job and shift to Mussoorie if she wanted to stay here. But she was firm. Must every love story end in marriage, she asked.'

'What did you say?'

'What did I say?' I repeated his question, trying to recall the exact words. 'I think I told her I was obsessed with the hope that someday we would go back to the university days. Sati was not convinced. She said that it only happened in movies. I assured her that it happened in real life too. She then informed me that she liked it there, amongst the girls. Every day for her was a surprise. As Sati is fond of exploring places, I asked her to travel with me. We could have gone to the beach, she always wanted to live by the sea! But she just shook her head. That was when I realized that a dream was just the feed for imagination.

'I have tried everything. I even added a letter to my name superstitiously. From Sat, I became Satt to match the number of letters in her name. But even that didn't work. Gradually, I accepted this decision of hers, as I have accepted all her wishes. There was only one time when I said no to her.'

'When?' they asked in unison.

'I don't know what got into her but one day when I went up to Mussoorie to meet her, she kept insisting that I should marry someone else. That was the only occasion when I walked away from her in anger. It had never happened before, nor ever since. That was also the last time she brought up the subject of me marrying some other person. She has now come to accept that we will both leave this world as we had arrived, single and unencumbered.'

The brothers were quiet. It was too poignant a moment to be spoilt by an unnecessary comment—even Shiv did not pipe up to make one of his silly remarks.

But words continued to pour out in a torrent from me.

'I wish I could hold her head in my hands,' I said. 'I would lower it gently to kiss her warmly on her forehead. Then, I might have the courage to tell her that she is wrong; that if we don't marry we will carry to the other world a trunk full of memories and a baggage of unfulfilled desires.'

I choked again; this time I did not make the effort to hold back my tears.

I kept crying for a long time; mostly in soft wordless sobs, but occasionally, it became a loud wail. Between sobs, I managed to add, 'I will also tell her that if by chance we were to marry, my greatest wish would be for our child to have eyes like hers.'

*T*hat was all there was to my story—my heartbreak and Sati's firm no. Since there was nothing more to add to this dead-end, we sat around awkwardly, thinking the same thoughts and wondering about my cruel fate.

I tried a joke to break the solemn spell. 'Did you guys hear this one?'

They looked at me politely.

But I carried on bravely. 'Why do you rob banks? This fellow asks. Because there is no money in the post offices, the thief replies.'

The joke fell flat and I did not try a second one after that. It was a poor joke, but even if I had told the world's best joke, it would be the wrong time. The news about Sati saying no to marriage had come as a terrible blow to the brothers and they were simply not in a mood for light banter.

Shyam was the more sensitive of the two. I could see from his tense muscle tone that he was trying to think of a way out of the mess that Sati and I had got into. 'It shouldn't end this way,' he murmured. 'There must be a way out.'

I shrugged my shoulders helplessly, and once again, we retreated into our private shells.

At last it was Shiv who broke the melancholy spell as a cold blast of wind tousled a group of clouds towards us. 'Can you see deep down in the valley?'

Shyam and I turned to look in the direction of his hand. 'Where?' we asked, unable to locate the object he had in view.

'There, you fools,' he gestured again towards the deep end of the valley. 'Have you chaps heard of Wordsworth?' he asked, his query laced with sarcasm.

'I know of Woolworth,' I said in another weak attempt at a joke.

'Had you read Wordsworth you would have spotted that bunch of flowers immediately,' Shiv scorned, pursing his lips. 'But illiterate, ignorant bums like you can only see trees. The flowers are beneath the trees like the daffodils of his poem.'

We noticed them then. They were not daffodils, but a big bunch of wild red flowers. And just like Wordsworth's daffodils, some of the red flowers were lying beneath the trees.

It was an idyllic scene, made more so by the fresh tufts of clouds gathering over the valley. Thus far, the cloud cover was sparse, there were still openings in their mushroom pattern for a beam to make its way through, and for the red flowers to shimmer.

A cloud broke free from that group and wandered towards us. It climbed the hill and jumped over the fence of the villa to hang low across the garden before covering us all in its vaporous mist. We luxuriated for a moment in that cottony wetness.

'Hey,' Shiv shouted to a servant, 'get me a stick.'

'What will you do with it?' Shyam asked.

'I will chase away that cloud with the stick.'

But the cloud had dissipated by the time a stick was produced. This was typical of the clouds that hung low in Mussoorie, especially those that crawled into someone's house. These intruders had a notoriously short life span.

Our tryst with them was not over yet because the valley below us was filling up with dark clouds again.

'Clouds bring depth to the sky,' Shiv said, apropos nothing at all.

He was the jester among us, providing endless entertainment with his quips. I was merely the master of the poor jokes. But jokes were not on the menu during our second night in Mussoorie.

Shyam usually set the mood in our meetings because he was the seniormost among us by a chronological whisker. I was the in-between man—younger to Shyam by one year, and a couple of months older to Shiv. That was why I usually got squashed between the two—in their arguments, and their barbs.

'I wonder whether we have ever told you why goras like us have Hindu names,' Shyam asked.

I chose not to respond, wondering if it was a trick question.

'You were too polite to ask,' Shyam continued in his baritone voice, 'but other friends have been direct. They are surprised at not just our Hindu names but also the fact that despite being suited-booted churchgoers we are also temple-going dhoti-walahs.'

'That's right,' I said for the sake of saying something.

'We are the goody goody Jekyll in the morning and the terrible Hyde at night.' Shiv butted in, 'Gora in the morning and Kala at night.' Then he shook his head and added on a politically correct note, 'Make it Kala in the morning and Gora at night. That sounds better, doesn't it?' he asked no one in particular.

Shyam gave him a withering look before carrying on as if he had not heard him, 'The reason for this double identity is very simple. Our parents were determined that if we are to stay in India we should be Indians in the real sense.'

'In the beginning, we were given Christian names,' Shiv chimed in again.

'Really?' I said, surprised by this new knowledge.

'My name was Sean, like Sean Connery,' Shiv replied. 'When I had to be Hinduised, Sean became Shiv.'

'And what was Shyam before he became Shyam?' I asked curiously.

'That was easy; you should have guessed it,' Shiv laughed. 'Sam became Shyam.'

This happened in an age when everything American was the rage in India. The young listened to rock music. They hero-worshipped Elvis by copying his Brylcreemed hair, his cocky walk, and the rakishly upturned collar of his shirt. It would certainly have been a plus with the girls if they had names like Sean and Sam.

'You people didn't object?' I asked.

'No, not really. As a matter of fact, the thought did not occur to us.'

'By having Hindu names we Christians became truly "sickular",' Shiv wisecracked.

'Sickular or secular?' I asked.

'It is one and the same thing, my friend.'

'This change wasn't just in our names. It also meant that we had to adopt an all-embracing faith in religions,' Shyam added. 'Christ and Krishna cohabited in our home. They were hung side by side on the same wall.'

'The other thing is that, despite the big bungalow and the servants, we weren't actually rich,' Shiv added.

I found this hard to believe. They had all the trappings of a reasonably rich family—a big bungalow, servants, a big car and the latest fashion in clothes. Moreover, the two boys had all the money to spend. I remember, in college, my pocket money used to run out by the third week of the month. But their wallets were seldom empty.

'We weren't rich,' Shyam said, 'but Ma knew how to stretch a penny and we liked to live well.'

'Live well and love well,' I whispered with a touch of envy.

here was a touch of bizarre to the situation. I had been the original lover boy; mine had been the greatest love story of the university. These two brothers were keener on sports rather than girls during their college days. Now they had become Casanova-like. Once people used to whisper my story in awe, now I was a mere sounding board; sometimes a patient listener of others' stories, and on other occasions, a teller of their tales—a sutradhar.

I have often asked myself why I did what I did. Why, when my own love life was barren to the point of non-existence, did I choose to be the mouthpiece for others? Or for that matter, why was I so interested in what they did inside their bedrooms?

Was it because of some perverse kick? Did their love stories represent a release for me, a catharsis? Or was it something more simple—a natural way of bonding when three friends met and wanted to have a good time talking about the things of the past. It could have been any of those reasons or a combination of them. My attempt to rationalize my role and find an answer left me feeling even more frustrated than before. But let me say with all honesty that I did not derive any vicarious pleasure by sharing other peoples' love stories.

If Mrs Keeling was alive, she would have reached over to sit next to me, and looking straight into my eyes, she would have asked, 'What's troubling you?'

I would pretend and say, 'Nothing. I am fine.'

But this would never fool her. She would put her hand over my forehead to smoothen my worry lines. 'Don't frown, otherwise they will become permanent lines,' she would scold gently.

Then she would pat my cheek and say, 'Nothing in the world is so important that it should worry you.'

There were countless other ways in which she made me feel special.

I remember clearly the first time when Sati had visited Mussoorie. Mrs Keeling had taken the two of us aside for a minute. Looking at us, she had spoken softly, measuring every word, 'The most cherished moment in a relationship is often the first, the initial revelation, when all of a sudden everything is open and obvious. That opening image remains etched forever in the form of a word, a sentence, the face, or the body. There will certainly be subsequent frames, they will superimpose themselves. Relationships may change. But the first impression remains, as a memory that soothes, as the first foundation of an edifice. Always keep it close to your heart.'

I was too young then to understand the subtle point of her comment, but I remember she had looked sad when she had turned to go into the house, as if she had a premonition of the twist in our tale.

'You were the last to meet her. What was she like then?' Shyam asked.

'She wasn't too bad physically. She had shrunk with age, about the same height as you two saw her on your last visit here. Her strength for small talk had reduced, but she was intellectually alive. She asked me questions and took notes.'

'Why?'

'I have no idea. Maybe for the book she was always busy writing. When I was about to leave, she said, "These days, I hold audience with my memory."'

'She loved life,' Shiv whispered, and his voice trailed off into the quiet night.

That was perhaps the best way to describe her—she loved life and she loved people. Mrs Keeling would have been happy to see us gather in her bungalow and talk of the old times. In fact, she needed no excuse to be happy, sometimes it seemed that she had been born with a smile permanently fixed on her face. There was just one thing that she had been unhappy about, and that was the issue of Sati and me.

She would talk about it every time we met, and constantly nag me to do something and marry Sati. The last time I had been here, I had reminded her of what she had told us about the first impression. Using that as a crutch, I had said, 'I carry her memory in my heart. It brightens the bleakest day. Even if we never marry, it is enough for me to think that she is beautiful. I can then paint her as I desire.'

But Mrs Keeling had not been convinced. She had shaken her head emphatically and had said, 'Memories are for really old people like me. You have to marry before you can think of having any memory of the other person.'

Had Mrs Keeling been alive, I would have told her that she was wrong. It was not necessary to be married to have memories of the other person. You could still long for her. And you could remember her with reason or without.

I remembered then the day Sati and I spent an entire day together; first at a debate where both of us were participating and which she had won by a wide margin. Then, we went out to lunch at the Moti Mahal restaurant outside the university campus. There, too, her choice of food was perfect, whereas my tandoori chicken arrived half-burnt. When I looked at it with distaste, Sati smiled sardonically and said, 'Looks are superficial. They are transient. You shouldn't go by looks.'

'Looks tell me this chicken is charcoal,' I snapped.

'You are mistaken. Look below the surface. You will then see the succulent flesh that lies beneath the burnt skin,' Sati responded. 'Tell me, would you have loved me had I been plain-looking?'

'That's silly.'

'No. It's not,' Sati insisted. 'I could catch a disease and end up with a horrible face. Would you not love me then?'

She did not wait for me to respond. Instead, she added sombrely, 'I know you wouldn't.'

Our table was placed in a little patch of green outside the restaurant. As she asked her question, she shifted in her seat and shook her hair. In the chaos of her curls, I saw sunshine. I knew then she was ribbing me just to have fun. So, instead of replying to her, I closed my eyes and smiled.

'Why are you smiling?' Sati asked curiously.

'When I'm nervous, I generally close my eyes and think of money. It is soothing,' I replied. 'But for the first time, when I closed my eyes, I saw your face. It freed me of all doubts.'

'Doubts?'

'So far, I had been looking for a black cat in a dark room. But when I saw the look of absolute serenity on your face, I realized I was chasing shadows.'

Sati turned to me sceptically, arching her eyebrows in enquiry. She wondered if I was being subversive on purpose.

'I think I am close to enlightenment,' I added, jolting Sati further.

'Really?' Sati crinkled her eyes and said, 'Close to enlightenment? Why just close? What eludes the great mind?'

'I worry about the consequences of greatness. What will happen to our relationship when I achieve enlightenment? I will be famous then; people will come from all over the world to see me and to seek my blessing. Will I have the time then for my personal affairs? Because great responsibility brings with it great uncertainty?'

'Tell me, what will you do with enlightenment if you finally get it?' she asked playfully. A dark strand of her jet-black hair danced teasingly across her face as she leaned forward.

It was at this point that I realized the aim of her circular rhetoric. She had done it on purpose to divert the conversation and to smoothen the wrinkles in our relationship. Left to fester, they could become irritants.

■

'I have never seen you look so despondent,' Shyam said sombrely. 'Remember, happiness is temporary. It is sadness that fills life.'

'For everyone?'

'Yes, for everyone,' Shyam asserted. 'In one way or the other, at one time or the other, we must suffer. That's the rule of life.'

I was not sure about everyone suffering, but I was sure I had suffered more than the average person's share of misfortunes.

'Be positive,' Shyam suggested, 'you can change your fortune by positive thinking.'

'I agree,' I replied. 'My problem is I know what to do, but every time gloom overwhelms me and I end up doing what I should not do.'

'Your problem is your past,' Shiv intoned. 'A past scarred by loss and hardship.'

I wanted to kick him, but the fact was that he was correct. I just could not shake off the past. For instance, this time, in Mussoorie, I found myself thinking increasingly of the Partition. Perhaps it had something to do with Mrs Keeling's death because the pain of her loss reminded me of the suffering I had witnessed as a child.

'There is this particularly bloody account,' I said. 'It continues to haunt me even after all these years.'

'Is it scary?' Shiv asked, half seriously.

'It is, for what it did,' I replied, before beginning my account.

twenty-eight

Sat

$\mathcal{O}$ ne afternoon, when I walked up to the tandoor, the chatter around it stopped abruptly. There was tension in the air. Men were gritting their teeth, their facial muscles taut. I could see from the way they were clenching and unclenching their fists that they had been discussing something sinister.

'Why did you stop?' one of the men asked.

The narrator turned towards me and said in a loud whisper, 'He is a child. He shouldn't hear such things.'

'Don't worry. He is too young to understand,' the people around him insisted. 'Tell us what happened.'

Hearing this, I was hooked; even at the young age of three, the forbidden excited me.

'It happened in the Raiwind village near Lahore,' the man began gravely. 'Hindus and Sikhs in west Punjab were a worried lot in the months before Partition. They were expecting a massacre any night because bands of Pathan and Baloch tribals were roaming the countryside looking for them. By way of an early warning, so that they could escape before the tribals arrived, every village had started keeping a volunteer on night watch. But in practical terms, this meant very little. Massacres followed relentlessly.'

The man narrating the account stopped to drink some water, but no one spoke or shuffled to break the silence. When he resumed, it was to an anxious audience.

'Late, one moonless night, the volunteer on guard duty at Raiwind heard a faint rumble in the distance. Then he heard the sound of guns being fired in the air and cries of animals scampering away. The guard started running, but before he could reach the largest house in the village, the faint rumble had become an approaching thunder of a hundred horses.

'The horsemen were identically clad in black salwar kameez and they had covered their faces with black scarves. The entire lot followed the guard to the biggest house in the village.

'Once there, they broke down the main door quickly, and rounded up all the hundred members of an extended Sikh family. Men, women and children were marched out of the house in single file, with their hands up. Outside the house, they were lined up against the perimeter wall.

'The man who was leading the raiders dispatched a team to torch the rest of the village. "Every single man, woman and child must be roasted alive inside the house," he instructed the party. Their flames rising in the night sky, he boasted, would make a great background for what was soon to unfold against the wall. As the tribal team was leaving on its macabre mission, he shouted after them, "Don't kill the young women. Bring them here with you."

'Then, he went down the line of people standing uncertainly against the wall. First, he separated the young women. They were to be taken away and raped. Next, he selected pregnant women. They were bunched together in a group at a little distance from the rest, but well within their sight. These pregnant women were stripped naked and their breasts were cut off one by one. When that first round was complete, they started again and sliced open the wombs to stifle the unborn. Every time, they cut a womb, they chanted, "Pakistan paindabad". The wails of the dying merged with the invocation for a new nation to produce a confused cacophony. The massacre happened, methodically and slowly.

'The men lined up against the wall were beheaded one by one so that the entire process could be seen by others who were going to survive a few minutes longer than the ones whose turn it was to face the sword. Their necks were not chopped off in one neat stroke, but in an excruciatingly slow and painful process. The killers called it halal—killing that is sanctioned.

'The sword lingered over the neck before it began to scrape the flesh like a very slow saw. The killers shouted "Pakistan paindabad" every time the first few drops of blood sprang out of a body. Meanwhile, the sword dug deeper into flesh, and blood began to flow in larger quantities. The squeals and the cheers of the murdering mass rang louder. They were celebrating death and they were doing so on purpose to drown the wails of the victim and the shrieks of witnesses.

'Every neck required a full two minutes of deliberately slow cutting. Exactly 120 seconds later, the neck fell to the ground. The killers were proud of their precision and readily accepted large bets for every second's variation. But each time, they were cruelly correct. Death arrived punctually every two minutes.

'One sliced head followed the other. At the end of two hours, all the male heads lay bleeding in a straight line against the boundary wall. The women had been bunched in a separate corner. One group lay bleeding on the ground, awaiting slow death. A second group consisted of young women lined up against the far end of the wall. This group was to be kept alive for the tribal leaders. They kept wailing, cursing their cruel fate.

'All this while, the killers were busy. They bundled the dead bodies in bullock carts, took them to a pond near Raiwind and dumped them all in it. Next, they rode back to the village to loot whatever there was to loot and to carry the young girls back with them.

'But unknown to them, there was a survivor in that lot. This little girl had escaped the mass murder. Luckily, her cries were heard the next morning by a passerby and it was he who brought her to Delhi.'

The man relating the story had the traumatized little girl by his side. She was about my age and I had wanted my parents to adopt that girl, but they were unsure about taking one more person in when their own meals were uncertain.

Even now, I get goosebumps when I think of her dumped

deep in the bleeding bodies of her relatives. I often wonder if she was ever able to erase that trauma, and whether she could ever reconcile herself to pardoning the killers. I never saw that girl again but I have prayed for her every single day of my life.

Those were grim times. There was savagery all around and it lasted for months. In those ghastly times, everything good about human nature had disappeared. All that remained was bitterness.

twenty-nine

'All that remains are dark memories,' Shyam said gravely. 'We Indians are a tolerant lot. We build new lives and carry on fatalistically.'

'But what is the alternative?' Shiv asked. 'If we seek revenge now, there will be more violence. Acceptance is the best policy.'

'Acceptance,' I repeated slowly, rolling the word over my tongue, like a wine taster. This one word excused every misadventure. But in our present condition, argument, rather than acceptance, was the preferred course. We were a boisterous and argumentative bunch that night. The excitement of being together and sharing our stories had made the liquor settle well. Moreover, we had been lacing our stomach with greasy food. So, all in all, we were pleasantly tipsy, and at best, mildly drunk. In that state of merriment, we were hoping the night would never end.

Our stories had been a mixed bag—some sad, others shocking, a few had even carried a touch of scandal, but each one of them was marinated in life's experience. Exchanging them had been the most civilized way of spending time together. That was why I said, 'Let me tell you another story.'

'You say you are not a historian, yet you remember everything. You claim modestly to be ordinary but you are a great sutradhar,' Shyam gushed admiringly. 'You are truly an artist; I wish you would get the recognition that's your due.'

'That's written in my stars,' I sighed resignedly. 'Some people do nothing, not a spot of work all their life, yet they walk on velvet all the time. They go from success to success effortlessly, people give them credit for what is not their due. In contrast, I have been knocking on closed doors all my life.'

'I might be saying so myself, but the fact is that I have worked hard and with the greatest sincerity in whatever job I have been assigned in office,' I added. 'Still, I am not one of those who attempt to shift the boundaries of destiny. I have rotten luck, but thank god I have another life beyond work where I try my hand at everything, from painting to singing, from conducting shows to telling tales. Everyone says I am a wizard at these things.'

'That you are,' Shyam said encouragingly.

'Yet all my hard work counts for nothing, because at the decisive moment, others step forward to take the credit. What right have others to take what is my due? I do not usually complain, but this injustice hurts. After all, I have feelings. I am sensitive, and every time someone else gets promoted it hurts me.'

'Oh!' Shiv said simply. This little interjection conveyed nothing, neither sympathy with my lot, nor satisfaction at my suffering.

'Sometimes I feel like the peacock who dances unseen and unappreciated in a forest. There was a time I used to feel very frustrated at this inequity, but I am reconciled to my fate now.'

'I don't think that's the case. People who know you know your worth,' Shyam said soothingly.

I looked pointedly towards Shiv. If he was of the same opinion as Shyam, he should have nodded, or at the very least, kept a straight face. But he made no effort to hide his smirk.

Then, for no reason at all, he slapped his thigh in great amusement. It was this sort of arrogance that I had always found annoying about Shiv. But in line with my recent resolve to not say anything that could spoil our evening, I said nothing at all. I merely smiled in abstraction.

But Shiv was not finished. 'Most promotions in the corporate world are based on merit,' he said.

'What is it that you have against Sat? Either come up with it or stop this nonsense at once,' Shyam's left eye began to twitch and his face reddened in anger. 'I thought we had settled it already. I don't want any more snide remarks.'

Shiv responded with a doubtful shake of his head.

'I wish I could be like a bull,' Shiv declared. 'I have a short list of people I want to gore.'

Shiv had vowed not to rib me, not just once but twice in the space of the last hour or so. Yet, he was at it again, hinting retribution for some unknown act of omission or commission by me. It was all very puzzling because Shiv had once been a gregarious and fun person.

I clenched my right fist so hard that nails began to bite into the flesh of my palm. Looking directly into his eyes, I said very slowly, 'Sati came here to Mussoorie on her own accord. It was her decision to join the school here and teach children.'

'You left her no choice. She thought it was the end of the road for her, the end with you, and your deceptions.'

'No,' I asserted, raising my voice. 'I proposed to her right here in Mussoorie, in the school canteen.'

The moment I said that, I knew it was a blunder. I had given Shiv another chance to rile me. Shiv burst out laughing, 'He says he proposed to her in the school canteen.' He mocked, 'And he actually expected her to swoon and say yes in front of the waiters. How unromantic can you get, Sat?'

I could not understand what was happening. Why was Shiv humiliating me? And why was Shyam quiet? He had never allowed Shiv to trash me in this manner before.

'What should I do?' I mumbled helplessly.

'How can I tell you what to do?' Shiv said. 'You are the great lover. You know everyone's stories. You have all the answers. Every time one of us tries to suggest something you cut us off by saying, "I know everything".'

I wish I had retaliated and said, 'Thank god I am not known by the company I keep.' I would have also liked to add that I was not a philanderer like him. He had chased every skirt in town whereas I had led an almost saintly life. Wasn't that sufficient penance for a lifetime? Had I not been punished enough for that single mistake of flying off to New York in a hurry?

Shiv's remarks were hurtful, but instead of hitting back, I

played the part of an injured soul—the helpless Raj Kapoor-like vagabond.

'Every woman dreams of falling in love at some point in her life,' I whispered. 'Above all, she imagines that her man should have a smile that lights up the room. What can I do if I am colourless?'

Shiv smiled. To me, it seemed like a silly smile, a self-congratulatory and mean smile—it meant that he was about to say something nasty.

Anticipating it, Shyam stepped in quickly, 'Sat, you have a problem. And it is simply this—you are naïve and too nice. The world is not cast in your image. Ideally speaking, that is how it should be. Everyone should be straightforward and simple. But that is not how it is. It is a complex world. Shiv is right in saying that a school canteen is not the right setting for lovers. You must choose better the next time, maybe engineer a dangerous situation.'

Shyam scratched his head. When inspiration struck him, he added triumphantly, 'You could go on a fragile bridge with Sati, or walk with her to the edge of a mountain when a fierce wind is blowing behind you. At that point, when her adrenalin flow is high, you should propose to her.'

'Bravo, that's exactly what I had in mind,' Shiv began promisingly before turning nasty again. 'This gives Sati a choice. If she doesn't want to say yes, she can push him down the mountain.'

Perhaps Shyam was right, perhaps even Shiv had a point in his perverse way, but they were simplifying a difficult situation. It was not a question of the perfect setting but one of the state of mind. It was true that Sati and I had been sitting in the canteen of her school when I had proposed. But no waiter had been hovering around us and there had been no dirty plate near us.

And the setting had been romantic.

Mussoorie would get very cold in December. That evening, the temperature was a couple of degrees lower than normal. When we exhaled, we could see the vapour on our breath move towards each other to merge as one. Earlier during the day, it had snowed almost continuously. But then, as we looked out of the window, we could see that the snowfall had thinned. We kept looking silently at the bleak landscape. Suddenly, Sati turned to me and asked, 'Did you say something?'

I was about to say no, but I changed my mind and said, 'I did, a long time back.'

Sati laughed, throwing back her head and tossing her hair. Her hair had spread open like a fan and she stretched her hands to tie them back with some ceremony. A strand of her hair strayed loose, irritating her.

'What did you say?' Sati repeated.

'We should marry.'

Sati was not expecting this so late in our lives. She looked up in surprise and watched me carefully to see if I was serious. Then, she smiled shyly, just as she used to in college.

As she used to do then, she spoke first through her eyes. There was a glint in those big upturned eyes. I began to hope again, but within those few seconds, she changed her mind again.

'It is not possible,' she said slowly, 'I am like a kite that wants to soar freely.'

'Please,' I urged, sliding my hand over the table to cover hers.

'Sat, you must understand that I have unfettered myself. Your love will restrict me.'

'Please,' I repeated helplessly, 'life offers only fleeting moments of happiness.'

'Where is the time? This lifetime is for me and for my mission to educate children.'

'What about our kids?' I asked, sensing a new opportunity.

Sati looked into my eyes, giving me new hope. Then, she smiled a sad smile, shutting the opening I had sensed just a moment back.

'My own kids are for my next life. In this lifetime, there is space only for me. My parents' lives were ruined because they exhausted themselves in bringing me up. They had no life of their own. Having children is a lifelong commitment. I love animals and other people's children too much.'

'We had dreams,' I pleaded.

'Dreams are just food for the imagination,' she replied.

This was a phrase I had often repeated to myself, but Sati wove words with such deftness that there was rarely any scope to turn them around in your favour. That was why she would win every debate she would take part in. Now, she was winning the debate of our lives.

After relating this account, I told Shyam and Shiv blandly, 'You can't say I didn't try.'

Shiv made a face, Shyam remained inscrutable as usual.

Meanwhile, at Mrs Keeling's house, the sky had turned ink

black. 'Look, there is lightning and thunder in the background,' Shyam remarked. 'The pack of clouds over us is dark and threatening. Even the jungle below is quiet. We haven't heard any animal sound for some time. This is a perfect setting for ghosts.'

I poured myself another drink, just in case.

thirty

'Greed is gorgeous,' Shiv remarked.

It was quite possible that he was referring to the extra-large drink I had poured. Or to the many girls in his life. But instead of reacting, I thought it best to deflect. 'It is, if you are lucky,' I said. 'Then everything is gorgeous—your greed and your loot as well.'

That was my rhetorical reaction. On a more serious note, however, the fact was that everyone in this world was greedy. It was not just the politician, the rich, or the ordinary; even the god-fearing could be greedy. You could also be greedy in love, for affection or just money. Those who had enormous amounts of money wanted some more. Those who didn't have any wanted lots of it. And it was not necessarily money that people always lusted for.

'You are a philanderer, a bloody serial philanderer. That's what you are,' Shyam snapped suddenly.

'Shyam,' Shiv warned.

'Don't you Shyam me,' Shyam shouted back.

'Girls outgrow me.'

'Girls outgrow me!' Shyam guffawed, imitating Shiv. 'Outgrow! Isn't that a convenient way of saying you discard them after using them?'

'Satisfied?' Shiv snapped in mock anger.

'And what is the result?' Shyam shot back snidely. 'Will your philandering ever end?'

'Must there be an end to every story? Some stories are told because telling them leaves you with a good feeling. Others are told by way of shedding skin, a sort of catharsis,' Shiv replied in an even tone. 'Now that you have heard all the stories about me, tell me, are you satisfied?'

'What is there for me to feel satisfied or dissatisfied about?' Shyam retorted.

'You tell me.'

'Let's not start it again,' Shyam said. 'I wish we could be together sometime without the arguments.'

Shiv was not in the mood to give up, 'You should ask yourself if you are satisfied with keeping everything a secret from me. Ma would have been horrified to see that I get to know about you from others.'

'Others! What do you mean others? Sat is not "others",' Shyam snapped. His eyes had narrowed as they usually did when he was angry, 'Sat was always Ma's favourite son. This was so from the beginning, much before the declaration you read in her computer.'

'So?'

'Sat is as much one of us as the two of us. Is that clear?'

Shyam continued sternly, pointing an accusing finger at him, 'Never ever say this again.'

But Shiv was not done yet. Soon he turned very mean again. 'Betrayal runs in his blood,' Shiv shrieked.

'What do you mean?' Shyam shouted back.

'Sat ran away from Sati. That is what I mean.'

'You are horrible,' Shyam snapped. 'Horrible and unfair.'

'Facts are facts,' Shiv said, holding his ground. This time, there was not even a hint of apology. He seemed to be provoking me on purpose.

In a situation like this, when I am very agitated, my head begins to throb with pain. It was even more painful to know then that I was the cause of this fight between the two brothers.

Shyam glared at Shiv but he did not say anything.

For a moment, as I watched their confrontation, I thought this was it—the prelude to a real explosion. It also seemed that my trick of diverting the conversation had not worked. But some higher force must have been at work because Shiv said sorry, the glaring stopped, and their eyes turned moist. Nothing more was said after that. This ability of mea culpa was the wonderful thing about the Keeling family.

I guess that was why I was so fond of them. And each time something like this happened, I would remember their parents because Mrs Keeling and her husband were the kindest people. It sounds almost too good to be true but they bore no ill will against anyone in the world. On the rare occasion that they had a grudge, they said so openly without rancour. Once they had cleared the air, the matter would be forgotten.

Generosity was their great quality. It was thanks to them that I could afford my college expenses. Mr and Mrs Keeling had sworn me to secrecy, even their sons never found out that they were helping me.

Still, I had issues with Shiv.

Once I thought I had heard him whisper to Shyam, 'Now what is it that Sat wants from us?'

I admit I never actually heard him say it in so many words, but from the way he had muttered through pursed lips and Shyam's scornful reaction afterwards, I could guess that he had said something to that effect.

It had hurt me, but I must also admit that if anyone needed help, the brothers were the people to turn to. Their hearts were as large as Mrs Keeling's bungalow.

$\mathscr{A}$ wolf was howling in the forest. The hoot had barely faded when the shrill sound of a whistle pierced through the night air, shaking us up. The sound of the whistle seemed to come from all around us.

At times it sounded distant, but a moment later, it came from behind us like wind rushing through the woods. Was it someone playing the flute? I wondered. But that was not possible because no flute could duplicate such an eerie sound. It was definitely not a human sound either, because no human being could hold his breath for so long. This whistle seemed to go on forever.

During our teens, we had been warned about such long-playing screechy whistles. It was believed that they were a prelude to the appearance of a ghost. Meanwhile, in the distance, at the other end of Mrs Keeling's garden, we saw a movement—a shadow seemed to be jumping across.

I drew my blanket tight around my legs. Shiv and Shyam stayed absolutely still in their chairs. Even their breathing was just about noticeable; that too if you paid very careful attention to the slight movement of their chests. They were drained of colour and made no move to shift in their chairs or adjust their blankets. Shiv looked deathly pale.

Suddenly, the whistling stopped almost as abruptly as it had started. As if on cue, a bolt of lightning lit up the night sky. In that instant, we saw a low-hanging cloud drift across the garden. That frisky cloud, rather than some ghost, was the reason we had seen a shadow jump. We began to breathe easy again.

It was now very late in the night, close to four in the morning when even the most alert guard tended to slacken a bit. Soldiers waited for this hour to strike at an enemy's military camp. Thieves called it 'the safe hour'.

To me, it was one of those nights when the whistle in the sharp wind carried evil tidings. In that eerie spell, I wanted to shut the world out for a while, to be left alone so that I could think of Sati.

When you are in love, every silence is a sacred space where no picture is complete and no single metaphor enough because a truly beautiful woman mirrors the harmony of creation. I began to think of a conversation I had with Mrs Keeling about Sati and myself.

I was sitting in my favourite armchair in her study, next to the window. The room was lined with almirahs, overflowing with books. Some magazines were piled up precariously on the floor. Mrs Keeling was sitting on a piano stool; she said it kept her body posture straight. We were drinking whisky and watching wood crackle in the fireplace. Normally, Mrs Keeling would have called out for soup after the second drink, but this time, she leaned forward and poured me another glass of whisky. I wondered what was up.

'You've waited all your life for Sati. Why are you so interested in her?' Mrs Keeling asked.

She could have asked why I had put Sati on a pedestal. Or said that there were other equally good-looking women in the world. But Mrs Keeling was discreet. Quite frankly, I did not have a clear answer as to why I had waited for Sati all my life. Perhaps it had something to do with the fact that we fell in love when we were in the first year of college. When you are young, you yearn for everything and believe in everything. Your head is full of ideas and what you see makes the heart throb. But what if you find all that and more in one person? Is there any need then to stray? Or even to think of someone else?

I had found everything in Sati.

So, asking me why I had waited for Sati all my life was like wanting to know why medieval monks spent enormous amounts of time trying to find out how many angels could dance on the head of a needle.

However, to Mrs Keeling, I said, 'You notice everything, don't you?'

'I notice everything about my children,' Mrs Keeling replied. 'But you have not answered my question. All your life, you have pursued Sati with the patience of a person climbing a long flight of stairs. Yet, you may never get to the top.'

'There are times when I wonder if my love for Sati is like worship for others. God is unobtainable for them, just as Sati is for me. On many other occasions, I feel like one of those young poets who are always in love with death and with the idea of love,' I said gently. 'I guess you can call it blind love.'

I coughed to clear a lump in my throat. 'Once, at the very beginning of our relationship, we had gone out for a walk around the university campus. By the end of it, the skies had darkened with thick clouds, the kind that makes people want to sing the latest Bollywood song.'

Mrs Keeling nodded knowingly, and gently took my hand in hers.

I continued telling her about that episode in our lives. 'Sati looked up and said, "You know, we've never had a hailstorm in Pune. I don't even know what snow looks like."'

'That night there was a hailstorm in Delhi. I woke up at three in the morning and went out to collect some hailstones from the hostel's lawn. I kept them frozen in the fridge till we met that afternoon. When I presented that packet of frozen raindrops to Sati, she laughed and said, "You fool!"'

'Good.'

'Then she leaned forward and gave me a kiss. Our lips touched for a few seconds only but it was enough to set off explosions in my head. It was the first time we had kissed, and I spent the entire week thinking about those few seconds.'

Mrs Keeling blinked to hide the moisture in her eyes. 'But still,' she remarked.

'I am a lot older now. But I think of Sati with the same intensity, with the same sense of helplessness. Even if I wanted to start another relationship, I wouldn't have the energy for the chase. I'm just not interested in someone else. As a matter of fact, the thought has never crossed my mind. After all these years, I continue to be enchanted by her.'

I thought a little and added, 'Enchanted is mild. Smitten may be more accurate.'

'I suppose happiness will come at the end of anguish,' Mrs Keeling remarked enigmatically.

'Yes, happiness is sweeter at the end of anguish,' I agreed.

Mrs Keeling chewed this mentally for a bit and then, as on so many occasions earlier, she came up wisely with the last word, 'Being able to cope with anguish is also happiness.'

I was thinking of this conversation with Mrs Keeling when Shyam shook me by the right arm and said, 'Where are you? Dreaming of Sati?'

'No, no,' I said quickly, 'just lost in a world of my own. But where were we?'

'Shiv has been waiting.'

'Waiting for what?' I wondered. Shiv was not the kind of person who would wait for anyone. He was more likely to break open a closed door to barge in.

'Shiv wants you to talk,' Shyam added.

'Why doesn't he talk himself?' I wondered. Normally, he would shout over everyone else to dominate a conversation. Why was he being polite now and actually asking me to talk?

'Sometimes, small little incidents can leave a deep impression,' Shiv said, anticipating my reservation. 'Such things are deeply personal and my reluctance to talk about them is because of my own confusion.'

'I am not sure what they represented,' Shiv shook his head, as if to clear his confusion.

It was not like Shiv to be confused about anything.

'Good, that for once you are confused,' I wanted to say. But I thought it better to avoid unpleasantness at this late hour, or rather so early in the morning, when a new day was about to begin. As a believer of omens, I was keen to have a positive start to the day.

---

thirty-two

*A*n early bird chirped. It was not dawn yet, but the dark night was giving way to a shimmer, which suggested that the daybreak was just the first sunray away. We had stayed up throughout the night without tiring of the effort, but it was becoming increasingly difficult to keep our eyes open now.

Had we been younger, we might have carried on for a few more hours. But we had exhausted all our stories. Moreover, this second night in Mussoorie had been one of amazing discoveries—of remembrance of the things of the past, and about secrets we had never shared earlier.

This long second night was our tribute to Mrs Keeling.

It was in her memory that we had exchanged stories throughout the night. Now we were sitting silently in the early morning chill, listening to the gurgling of water in the fountain. Earlier, just an hour or so ago, heavy clouds had rested on the pine treetops. They, too, must have listened to our stories. But they had scattered the moment we had stopped telling them. We were now watching wondrously the passage of the last bits of thin slivers of clouds across the face of the moon. To us, they seemed like carelessly shredded veils. There was no need for conversation anymore. We kept listening to the chirping of crickets instead.

We had already spent a day together in Delhi followed by two days in Mussoorie. The plan now was to sell the property within the next day or two and go our separate ways.

God alone knew when we would be together again. But these few days had been intense and immensely enjoyable. I also realized that, in our old age, we had developed the ability to compress time and accommodate the past. We could, thus, rationalize and remember only the good parts, the parts where we laughed and had a riot.

We had been friends for long enough to make out that each one of us was thinking roughly the same thought, that this second night would stay with us for a long time. We were also conscious that all three of us might never meet and bond like this ever again in our lives. None of us were looking forward to saying goodbye forever.

It was Shiv who broke the silence, 'There is a market in Varanasi where you can buy a ghost.'

Shyam and I exchanged glances, one could depend on Shiv to provide a silly diversion.

'I am serious,' Shiv said, reading our thoughts. 'Women who are possessed are asked to display their powers at this auction market. People can buy them outright or rent them for a period.'

'We have enough ghosts of our own in Mussoorie. Why should we get one from Varanasi?'

Shiv, as usual, was quick to respond, 'One of the many effects of Mussoorie is to set one longing; the mountains and valleys here make you want more of the same, more trees, more flowers, more clouds, more sunshine, more food and more ghosts too. So, an extra ghost can always be accommodated here.'

By that frivolous comment, he was trying to snap links with Mussoorie because once they were back in New York and London, they would be in a different world. That was not the case with me. I was going to go back to sultry Delhi where faces glistened with sweat in heat and peoples' spectacles kept sliding down their noses. Out on a Delhi road, you could witness the depressing spectacle of men hanging like swarming bees out of a bus door, clinging to its handle and to each other. That sight of sweaty bodies rubbing against each other in the 45-degree heat was the most distasteful part of Delhi's summer.

'If you had one wish, what would it be?' Shiv asked me.

I didn't respond.

Why did he want to know about my ultimate wish? Was it some devious scheme to pry out my most intimate secrets? Did he want to ambush me when I was dead tired? A number of negative thoughts came to me in a torrent—our iffy relationship and his interest in Sati.

My instinctive reaction was to ignore the question and avoid his intrusive interest. But on second thoughts, I decided that it would be unfair to Mrs Keeling and to my kinship with him. Shiv was a brother to me, and so was I to him, despite our filial rivalry. There was, therefore, no question of ignoring him, or his question.

Still, I couldn't resist taking a swipe at him.

'If you were to break the habit of a lifetime and look at the bright side,' I spoke slowly, stressing each word, 'then you will not ask people their dying wish.'

'Every time I try to make up, you crush me with your sarcasm,' Shiv bristled. 'Why can't we ever have a normal conversation? Don't I have the right to ask you something? Or should we just exchange polite nods with each other every time we meet, if we meet at all now?'

'Stop it, please,' Shyam intervened.

'Next time, whenever that is, I will just talk to you about the weather.'

'Enough, let's be sensible,' Shyam admonished.

'Why should only I be sensible? Why don't you ever ask him to be sensible?' Shiv said, jabbing a finger at me. 'You will never do that because he is your favourite brother.'

Shyam did not react, but he urged me to respond to Shiv's query.

I shook off the shawl and got up from my chair in a huff. For the next ten minutes, I kept pacing up and down the garden. After I had calmed down sufficiently, I returned to my chair.

I could not say no to Shyam. After all, there had never been any tension between us. In the end, I also decided to honour Mrs Keeling's memory—she would not have liked unpleasantness dividing us.

'Okay, as you say,' I said, looking at Shyam. 'My wish, my one and only wish, will be to see time in a rewind. I wish I could go back to those days and months when I had first met

Sati. You may well ask me why, and my reason for it is simple. My most cherished moment of life was the initial revelation when all of a sudden everything became clear. The first word, those first sentences, that first look—all those remain etched in my memory. Everything about Sati is memorable, but that first impression is special.'

I cleared the lump in my throat before continuing, 'If I could have a sequel to that wish then I would also want time to stop at the point when I saw her again after so many years. I had hoped that maybe this time she would lower her face and turn up those big eyes shyly to say "yes".'

It took great effort on my part to say all that. Having got it off my chest, I sank back heavily into my chair.

thirty-three

$\mathcal{W}$hat I did not add was the fact that I was riddled with self-doubt. When I would wake up at night, and it was often that I did, I would worry about her. Her penance troubled me. Even after all these years, I could not understand the reason she had chosen to become an ascetic. I kept asking myself repeatedly, where and how much had I slipped up? Was there some way things could have been different?

Perhaps, they might have been if I was not polite like my father. But I have always been a respecter of rules, so I had rushed out of jail to catch the first flight to the USA because the new academic session was starting there. Had it been someone else, someone brasher, he would not have gone to New York on the scheduled date. Instead, he would have gone to Pune first to meet Sati.

I had been paralysed by the same diffidence when I met her in the school canteen. I had failed to press her enough. I had simply stated my case, made my request, and had hoped for the best. That was no way to change a lady's mind. But that was how I was—always considerate, forever humble, and constantly mindful.

That, unfortunately, was not how battles of hearts were won. I felt sorry for my condition, but even sorrier for Sati, because she must have been terribly lonely in that sanctum-like girls' convent. And I knew from my own suffering that the root of all complexities in life was loneliness. That was the reason why her silence had troubled me so much when we had met at the tea shop.

After every meeting, I would kick myself in frustration and ask, 'Was our love only a three-minute tango where I kept my eyes firmly shut?' I would also ask myself if I was the same person who had dreamed of changing the world, a person who had plenty of time on his hands to do all this but who could not make an effort when it was needed the most.

I wish things had turned out differently.

'I know exactly what you are going through,' Shyam remarked ponderously.

'I don't know what I am going through. My heart is calm now, but I pine for her all the time.'

'It might be different if you did not drink every day. I know you drink in moderation, just one or two. But alcohol adds to the anxiety,' Shyam suggested.

'I drink to escape memories. But poor Sati, she can't even do that. She has no family and no friends, just the abstemious nuns to keep her company. Sometimes I feel that they could be a restricting influence on her, advising her not to fall for the temptation of marriage. I worry for her even more when she lapses into melancholy silences.'

I should have added that I missed looking deep into her eyes on a moonlit night. I longed to see moonbeams dancing in those big round eyes.

RAJIV DOGRA

The first rays of sun glided in from over the hill and we got up to bathe. At breakfast, the conversation was desultory; the occasional rustle of a newspaper or a request for passing the salt broke the silence.

Shiv was the first to get up. 'Better hurry up,' he said, addressing no one in particular. 'We leave in half an hour.'

This was unexpected. He should have given some notice, he could have told me before we went in for our bath that we would leave shortly after breakfast. This was too abrupt, as if I counted for nothing. But I didn't say anything. I went in quickly to my room and packed my bags. When they had been placed in the car, I noticed mine were the only ones in it!

Was Shiv playing some trick on me? Or did he simply want to get rid of me so he could spend some quality time with his real brother?

Shiv and Shyam came out together. They had some papers with them, but there was still no sign of their luggage. I also felt a bit slighted when they slid into the backseat of the car and waved at me to take the front seat. On our way up from Delhi, we had all snuggled up together in the backseat.

This time, I did not seem to exist.

All the while, on the way to wherever they were going, they kept exchanging confidences in hushed whispers, and they double-checked their papers endlessly. When the car stopped, I noticed that we had reached the land registration office. Since they had not bothered to tell me, I chose not to ask why they had come there. But I assumed that they had found a buyer for the house.

A property agent met them there. 'Everything is arranged,' he told them airily with a wink. 'The formalities won't take more than ten minutes.'

Shiv told me curtly to wait under a tree in the courtyard. I noticed apprehensively that it was a tamarind tree—the tree that people in the hills believed to be cursed by ghosts, the tree that they associated with certain death. Still, I did as I was told and looked on sullenly as they disappeared into the corridors of the registration office.

While I waited, I reminisced about our two nights in Mussoorie. The first night, as in the first night of a marriage, had passed by in a rush. The second night had turned out to be amazing, though slightly risqué. I had thought I alone would end up providing sketches from my life. But all of us had revealed more of each other than ever before in our lives. But why had Shiv spoiled it by being step-motherly towards me?

Meanwhile, they were done with their work at the registration office. They emerged precisely ten and a half minutes later and

Shiv shoved a set of papers under my nose and told me gruffly, 'Sign them.'

'Why should I?' I wanted to slink back and ask. There was also the fear that by signing a document that I had not read, I might be getting into something nasty. After the way Shiv had behaved with me over the last few days, I simply did not trust him.

But Shyam stepped forward and said, 'Please.'

This was different—I just could not refuse Shyam. Reluctantly, I took out my pen and signed wherever Shiv wanted me to. But I was so upset with him that I didn't even bother to look at the papers he was asking me to sign. I just wanted to get it all over with, quickly. I had already resolved that this was the last I would ever see of Shiv.

The agent took the papers and soon returned with them to inform us that the formalities were completed. Then, for no reason at all, he shook my hand.

From the registration office, we drove back to Mrs Keeling's bungalow. When I enquired about leaving for Delhi, Shiv replied dismissively, 'Later, we will tell you when.'

This was very rude of Shiv. 'We will tell you when'—as if I was their hired hand. I ignored the provocation.

We went in straight to the dining room where a guest was already seated. Her back was turned towards us.

'Noooh!' I gasped.

But Shyam and Shiv were already shaking her hand and hugging her with tears in their eyes.

Finally, it was Shyam who turned towards me and waved

his right hand in my direction as if to introduce me. 'Meet the new owner of this bungalow,' he said simply.

'I am what?' I protested.

'The new owner. You just signed the papers.'

'But that's not right. You both should be the owners, no one else. Whose idea was it?' I blabbered.

'Shiv's,' Shyam replied.

'Shiv's?'

'It was Shiv's idea right from the beginning,' Shyam confirmed. 'After hearing about Sati being here, there was no way we could let you go back. It is goodbye to Delhi as far as you are concerned.'

'Don't fly away to New York again,' Shiv added softly.

Sati lowered her face and smiled shyly.